The Unwritten Book

THE UNWRITTEN BOOK

An Organic Personal Conscious Evolution

SUZANNE F. HUBBARD

Waterside Productions

Copyright © 2021 by Suzanne F. Hubbard

All rights reserved. This book or any portion thereof may not be reproduced or used in any manner whatsoever without the express written permission of the publisher except for the use of brief quotations in articles and book reviews.

Printed in the United States of America

First Printing, 2021

ISBN-13: 978-1-951805-86-9 print edition
ISBN-13: 978-1-951805-87-6 ebook edition

Waterside Productions
2055 Oxford Ave
Cardiff, CA 92007
www.waterside.com

Dedication

Who is willing to stand by…
While you die a hundred deaths
And you keep picking yourself up?
My sister Woodleigh
Has walked this journey with me.

Acknowledgements

The soil, ecosystem, and birthing are the metaphors I wish to use to acknowledge individuals who played an important role in the development of this book. My children, Peter Hubbard and Renée Brown, and husband, Sandy Brown, provided the nurturing soil where it took root and grew. Ideas and wisdom from my late mother, Barbara Marx Hubbard, and dear friend the late Jacqueline Baldet were the ecosystem where my insights thrived. The soil and ecosystem nurtured and gestated the book through a period of pristine silence, but once I finished the manuscript, the midwives and partners stepped in to assist with preparing it for birth. Editor and friend Nancy Morgan showed sensitivity to what was being born while ensuring its message would be communicated clearly. Joshua Barwick and Reverend Carla Pryne read the manuscript and their feedback ensured what I am communicating will be understood. Without a book publisher, illustrator, and cover designer, the book could not have come into form. What the baby might look like remained a mystery until illustrator Steven Noble and graphic artist Kristine Dahms revealed its captivating personality. Publisher Bill Gladstone and Senior Publishing Associate Joshua Freel showed immense patience and assurance that the baby would, indeed, be born.

My heartfelt thanks for each of your contributions—I deeply appreciate you all.

Table of Contents

Introduction xi

Part One: Evolutionary Perspective 1
Chapter I   Our Great Mystery 3
Chapter II   Story-Mirror Jacqueline Baldet 14
Chapter III   Story-Mirror The Snowstorm 20
Chapter IV   Story-Mirror Peter and Renée 27

Part Two: Conscious Evolutionary Perspective 35
Chapter V   The Evolutionary Crossroads 37
Chapter VI   Conscious Evolution 41
Chapter VII   Organic Conscious Evolution 48

Part Three: Coevolutionary Perspective 53
Chapter VIII   The Rhythm of Outer and Inner Gardening 55
Chapter IX   Conscious Evolutionary Gardening:
                 The Seven Garden Chores 59
Chapter X   Conscious Evolutionary Gardening:
                 Tapestry of Thought 70
Chapter XI   Four Woven Swatches 81
Chapter XII   Conscious Evolutionary Weaving 85
Chapter XIII   Conscious Evolutionary Weaving: Mystical
                 Thought-Strands 100
Chapter XIV   Unifying Our Universal Masculine and
                 Feminine Principles 106

Chapter XV   Upper Fabric: Immaculate Universal Self-
    Conception Sex-Ed Primer: Imagining with Nature 113
Chapter XVI   Lower Fabric: A Universal Self-Conception 122

About Suzanne..133

INTRODUCTION

Becoming who we truly are could make all the difference in the world.

I join a growing family of individuals who are, at this point, desperately trying to preserve, protect, and change what appears to be a relentless human assault on the planetary system on which all life depends. Ecologists, naturalists, activists, conservationists, educators, politicians, artists, and many more are raising their voices and taking action. I wish to contribute with a perspective on what could be the latent human potential to coevolve. In other words, a solution to problems being caused by independent ways of life could be discovering what would innately inspire becoming interdependent. Nature may be experimenting with a species who can become universal self-conscious and guided. The experiment will fail unless we choose to respond. The purpose of this book is to support making this choice by identifying how we are personally experiencing the call to coevolve.

In the same breath that I completed this book in early 2020, the pandemic – the novel coronavirus, COVID-19 – emerged and is threatening our collective ability to breathe. The rhythmic inhale and exhale cycle of the breath, which sustains life, is also what unifies each to the other and everything with the shared larger whole. *The Unwritten Book: An Organic Personal Conscious Evolution* is timely as it embraces a biological and spiritual truth—we are all connected.

An Australian Aboriginal elder offered a humanizing wisdom to address the devastating wildfires in his country: "The greatest thing we have to offer today is our humanity, because this is all we ever had." Homelessness, the opioid crisis, global warming, and economic, racial, and social inequalities – all forms of oppression and exclusionary offensiveness – can only be possible when one believes all are separated and unrelated. The Unwritten Book cultivates, weaves, and gestates this biological and spiritual truth with the help of one's own deepest impulse and attraction to see, be, and become who we truly are.

Part One

Evolutionary Perspective

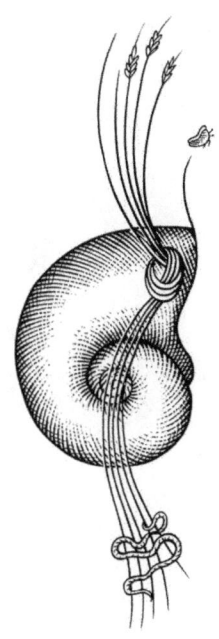

Chapter I
Our Great Mystery

Who are we before we become the person we identify with? Rarely is this question asked but there is a good reason, while it is not uncommon to sense and feel we have a truth that is universal and unknown. What this could be has remained a mystery, but it is felt whenever we are fully seen and heard. What is seen and heard, however, is never for the person we identify with. Instead, it is a resonant experience of a shared universal self or common ground that unifies. Although essential, this transcendent self-awareness is also down to earth. There is another part to it. A desire to know what it means and to speak its truth is a human emotional response. It links the transcendent with the everyday. Nevertheless, these are usually dismissed as foreign and inconsequential to the world we live in.

The transcendent and intimate experiences compose one universal self-awareness. It is a revelation expressing *all is one* and it is also known by a desire to identify with the larger whole and to live the unitive truth. If the transcendent awareness is mysterious, it would make sense that responding to a palpable desire-prompted / process-based impulse and attraction is how one may discover what it is. In other words, our instincts and emotions provide inner guidance. Choosing to respond, because we live in a world that evolves independently, would automatically make transitioning to environments that coevolve, an uncharted wilderness. Similarly, the effect of participating, which humans have yet to embrace as *the work*, is an untold story—what is possible has remained enshrouded in mystery. An imaginary line, separating independent and interdependent ways of life, has rarely been crossed. Responding would simultaneously: lift the veil on a missing human face, as it would fit us into a co-organizing planetary system, while at the same time, we would also be transforming it. The destructive force of a pandemic has pushed us to the edge of an unknown future. Could heightened individual awareness plus integrated personal / universal expression influence a future that could mirror its wholeness?

Our simple givens – to be human, to be alive, and to have a life – are low-tech mediums whereby a message is revealed to us: all is one. There is a possible ecological explanation. Environmental philosopher Baird Callicott explains the universal truth for all species, including ours.

> Ecological science focuses attention on relationships. It reveals that organisms are not only mutually related; they are also mutually defining. A species is what it is because of where and how it lives. From an ecological view, a species is the intersection of a multiplicity of strands in the web of life. It is not only located in its context, *it is literally constituted by its context.*[1]

A transcendent universal self-experience compares to the ecological view—we are mutually related and mutually defining. It seems obvious that the desire-prompted / process-based impulse is Nature calling us to live its message by identifying with a universal self. Could a full response to the innate understanding be how we join the rest of the living world?

Physicist David Peat acknowledges that people throughout the ages have known we have a relationship with the universe. It has

---

1 Frances Moore Lappe, *Diet for a Small Planet* (expresses Baird Callicott's viewpoint), (New York, NY: Ballantine, imprint of Random House, 1991), *xxvi*.

remained unknown, which thus means we are also a mystery unto ourselves.

> Each of us is faced with a mystery. We are born into this universe, we grow up, work, play, fall in love, and at the end of our lives, face death. Yet in the midst of all this activity we are constantly confronted by a series of overwhelming questions: What is the nature of the universe and what is our position in it? What does the universe mean? What is its purpose? Who are we and what is the meaning of our lives?[2]

There are many who would prefer to let this mystery be. Understanding it, however, could be a solution to the problem of humans remaining removed from Nature's world of participatory relationships. As incredible as it may seem, according to scientists such as Walter Alvarez, our ways of life have become the *force* that is pushing the sixth mass extinction.

> *We're seeing right now that a mass extinction can be caused by human beings.*[3]

Extinctions are a fact of geologic life and what has caused them in the past has differed. The end-Ordovician extinction, for example, was prompted by glaciation and the end-Permian extinction, 252 million years ago, was due to climate change when temperatures rocketed to a level that warmed the seas by as much as eighteen degrees. Sixty-five million years ago, a six-mile-wide asteroid crashed into earth, triggering the end-Cretaceous extinction.[4]

---

2 Ervin Laszlo, *Science and the Akashic Field: An Integral Theory of Everything*, cites David Peat (Rochester, VT: Inner Traditions, 2004, 2007), 2.
3 Elizabeth Kolbert, *The Sixth Mass Extinction: An Unnatural History* (New York, NY: Henry Holt, 2014), 104.
4 Ibid.

Dutch chemist Paul Crutzen, who shared the Nobel Prize for discovering the effects of ozone-destroying compounds, has dubbed our age the "Anthropocene." It means "the age of man"'—referring to separated lifestyles that destabilize the entire planetary system. He wishes to warn us that we must live differently. By calling our age the Anthropocene, Crutzen intends to

> ...focus our attention on the consequences of our collective actions—and hopes we might still avert the worst. "What I hope," he says, "is that the term 'Anthropocene' will be a warning to the world."[5]

The increasingly industrialized world thinks rationally. Its views do not include input from our instincts and emotions and thus lack critical self-awareness; were it to be responded to, the problem of independent objectives and lifestyles would resolve. The stumbling block with the dominant thought process is that it relates by comparing, contrasting, and separating. Unintentionally this instills the belief: all is separated. Our world has become a victim of the effects of how we think—rationally. Systemic racism and implicit bias, for example, are mirrored reflections of unintegrated thinking which leaves out instinctual and heart-felt universal self-awareness. Gnostic scholar Jacob Needleman homes in on the issue at hand. We have become unmoored from the root of subjectivity where pure instinctual and heart awareness are instilling and guiding appropriate actions. They are inspired by a human intuition or gnosis: we are essentially or ecologically the same as everyone and everything else. Even Greek philosopher Plato, more than 2,000 years ago, questioned whether everyday thinking should be considered a legitimate knowledge.

---

5 Elizabeth Kolbert, "Enter the Anthropocene Age of Man" (Seven Billion Series), *National Geographic Magazine,* March 2011, 77.

But it is the notion of gnosis as transformational knowing that is of utmost importance and that cries out for deeper inquiry in the world we now live in, a world – a civilization – which is deeply, perhaps fatally, afflicted with an ever-widening disconnect between what we know with the mind and what we know in our heart and in our instincts.

Both in our civilization and in our personal lives, the growth of knowledge far outstrips the growth of being, endlessly complicating our existence and taking away from us far more than it gives us. In relation to the advances and applications of scientific knowledge, we are like children restlessly sitting at the controls of a locomotive. Without a corresponding growth of inner, moral power, our intellectual power seems now to be carrying us toward disaster— in the form of the catastrophic destruction of the natural world, in the decay of ethical values, in the secrets of biological life falling under the sway of blind commerce or blind superstition, and above all, in the impending worldwide nuclear terror. May we not therefore say, as Plato said 2,500 years ago, that such 'knowledge' as we have does not really deserve the label 'knowledge.' Can we listen to him as he tells us that knowledge without virtue can neither bring us good nor show us truth?[6]

Thumbs, standing upright on two feet, our big brains, and the ability to problem solve and cooperate are human developments that are viewed as having evolutionary significance. What has yet to be considered in the same light is the ability to become universal self-conscious and guided. This intuition mirrors feedback from our instincts and heart, which when responded to, integrates a mind, body, heart gnosis, bringing a radical change in a world that views everything as separate. Switching over to an integrated

---

6   Jacob Needleman, foreword to *The Gospel of Thomas* by Jean-Yves Leloup (Rochester, VT: Inner Traditions, 2005), viii.

experiential and intellectual lens could revive an ailing civilization, when responding is how life can act through us. Becoming multi-perceptually universal self-aware is how the future could mirror the vitality of this understanding. Responding is also how to heal the many destructive impacts of separated thinking, such as influencing a mass extinction. It is also how we participate interdependently with our surrounding, which Baird Callicott explained is *both* the all-sustaining web of life, *and*, we are literally constituted by its context.

The Unwritten Book refers to *the wisdom of the unwritten book of life*, which captures the potential of an integrated mind, body, heart synthesis to relate interdependently rather than separately. To make this connection will require an entire set of new perspectives based on personal history of mysterious impulses and attractions.

Your LifeBook Journal, appearing at the end of each chapter, is a book-wide contemplative journaling process, where your threads of unconsciously responding become woven into your *evolutionary, conscious evolutionary, and coevolutionary perspectives*. Together these relook at the meaning of life from the experience of, again to refer to Baird Callicott, *being the intersection of strands* in the web of life. Each Part of the Unwritten Book uses the LifeBook Journals for multi-perceptually integrating inner and outer understanding of an ecological truth: we exist in the fabric of life and each of us is a unique expression of the whole.

Part One unearths an evolutionary subtext to personal histories, where in the midst of living the normal independent existences, there is an unconscious response to instinctual and emotional cues to live aware of the oneness of life. We come into the world compelled to live its experience in our unique way—this is identified as a *golden thread calling*. It is encoded with our own version of the wisdom of the unwritten book. Its attraction is deeply personal, but its impersonal purpose is equally relevant to ecological integration and social transformation. A correlation exists between a unitive consciousness and a related conscience which acts responsibly in addressing social injustice and climate change—both being byproducts of the unintegrated mind. Surrendering is a love-guided pathway for becoming integrated holograms of the web of life or shared universal self. There is an impersonal aspect to knowing who we truly are by following our heart's golden thread desire. As we live interdependently, we become a positive force of evolution. The chapters are *story-mirrors* that catch glimpses of what the future could look like, were we to live universal self-conscious. For example, our needs could be met more easily when life can flow through us. Acting on a sense and feeling of unity is how to reap the rewards of living interdependently. Strands from your evolutionary history are harvested and become woven into the fabric of a personal *evolutionary perspective* in Part One of Your LifeBook Journal.

Part Two begins with a look at the sixth mass extinction as it relates to chaos theory, which includes the phenomenon called a *chaos window*. Theorist Ervin Laszlo, however, refers to it as a *human decision window*. Disconnected lifestyles have paved the way to destabilizing the entire planetary system. Humans have played a role in causing this event. He shows that we also play a pivotal role in influencing the direction that evolution will take. It could be devolutionary if we choose to do nothing. On the other hand, if we act on the handwoven evolutionary perspective from Part One, it could catalyze real transformational effects.

Part Two supports developing a conscious evolutionary perspective; what it takes to fully respond to the harvested strands of universal self-feedback becomes transparent, a clear choice. When the instinctual and emotional golden thread callings have rarely been taken seriously, this transition – from the familiar linear perspectives and objectives to ones multi-perceptual and love-guided – will entail a major voluntary personal adjustment.

A conscious evolutionary perspective, therefore, is needed to support interdependent thinking-with and living-with the world around us. Trust and faith in the call could be how we move safely through the human decision window into a future we want to live in. A conscious evolutionary choice to become universal self-conscious and guided could be the key that unlocks the window's shuttered casement. Without a perspective, our instinctual and love-guided responses to global warming and social chaos will remain unconscious and thus unavailable for making decisions.

Matt Richtel writes in *An Elegant Defense: The Extraordinary New Science of the Immune System—A Tale in Four Lives*[7], the following account of our immune system's primary concern. "Survival depends on knowing what is self and what is alien." He then describes how it succeeds to protect us: "It walks the most delicate path. It succeeds with the help of peacekeepers so effective that their work could be mistaken for magic." Although he is referring to pathogens and viruses as "alien," while our own cells are self, I see parallels between protecting our personal well-being as well as others' and the natural environment as depending on recognizing *what is the universal self* and *what is the alien separated self*.

Could surviving the physical and existential threats being posed by the pathogen coronavirus include responding to multiperceptual understanding of what is the true self and what is alien? Could a choice to surrender to the unanimously love-inspired gnosis – we are unique expressions of the same universal self – become a healthy immune response to a deeply divided world? Could our love-guided golden threads reweave a social fabric, ensuring the well-being of the whole?

Novelist and activist James Baldwin gives an example of the miraculous effects of imagining with your heart rather than remaining influenced by separated Western (white-people) thinking. The "Negro" problem, as is also true of all trauma due to unresponsiveness to intimate universal self-awareness, *would no longer be needed*.

> White people in this country will have quite enough to do in learning how to accept and love themselves and each other, and when they have achieved this – which will not be

---

7   Matt Richtel, *An Elegant Defense: The Extraordinary New Science of the Immune System* (New York, NY: HarperCollins, 2019), 55.

tomorrow and may very well be never – the Negro problem will no longer exist, for it will no longer be needed.[8]

Might a mass extinction, too, no longer be needed, for the same reason? Part Three supports following through with a love-guided decision to become integrated with the perspectives of three organic personal conscious evolutions. *Conscious evolutionary gardening, inner weaving,* and *unifying universal masculine and feminine principles*—these all use a personal impulse and attraction to guide the multi-perceptually intuitive conscious evolutionary focus. Gardening, weaving, and gestating are human activities—fractals of patterns of interdependent relationships. The analogies offer a non-verbal or non-subjective context for instinctively and sensually relating to our larger whole, involving a natural rhythm and cycles of conscious evolutionary healing and expanding. This is a human understanding that is unobstructed or influenced by the biases of thinking separately.

The primary challenge I have faced writing this book is: it is based on "what if" we made the decision to passionately and compassionately coevolve? Transcendent and desire-prompted / process-based universal self-impulses and attractions are as mysterious today as they ever were. I weave tapestries of thought to add structure to understanding the transformations that are possible. Individuals can choose (conscious evolution) to heal personal trauma from being misunderstood (for who we truly are); they also can decide to trust and have faith in the call. The thought-strands are woven with neurological, ecological, biophysical, quantum mechanical, and mystical perspectives.

The different intellectual textures of the thought-strands are critical for understanding the evolutionary significance of becoming who we truly are. Science describes *what is*—which when mystically expressed becomes the being That Is What It Is, the I AM that

---

[8] James Baldwin, "Letter From a Region in My Mind," Nov. 17, 1962, *The New Yorker Magazine*, Dec 3, 2018, 32.

calls me to be. Making connections, a personal relationship with the larger whole, could change the question from *what if,* to *why not choose to surrender?* Scientific and mystical memes, which may appear separate, will be used here as mirrors for seeing how we are personally experiencing what they are describing. An intimate reference to our relationship with What Is therefore is most compelling. The perspective of a sum of interwoven mystical and scientific thought-strands, along with threads of personal experiences, could be a synthesis that serves as a bridge. Might we be able to cross the invisible line, where most people stop responding and rarely budge an inch? Migrating across are the adventure, the focus, and history that will be imagined in the Unwritten Book.

Our life could take on the living textures and tactility of a coevolutionary experience with fluid choices to respond and imagine multi-perceptually. A seagull is an animated expression of her ecosystem. Multi-perceptual universal self-awareness could be how we too express the larger whole—not as a separate identity, but rhythmically, dynamically, and inclusively. There may be wont of perspectives that clarify our relationship with the universe and yet we do have one. It is therefore to discover how we are relating and use this history to weave the threads of an intimate personal understanding.

Your completed LifeBook Journal is a pioneering book of records. It documents a distanceless conscious evolutionary journey from the world of the separated mind, which has been turned upside down by a virus and increased social paralysis, to a possible interdependent world we all see and live in. This unknown destination unfurls as its fabric is woven with a passionate and compassionate impulse and attraction to see, be, and become who we truly are—not for ourselves only, but the good of the larger whole.

~ Your LifeBook Journal

Recall your sense of mystery. Have you known this as a wistful fantasy or is it a poignant desire to know what it means? A passion to discover becomes a notch—a deep mountain pass, through which breezes scented with coevolutionary adventure and a whiff of freedom could fill your sails. Can you make a rite of passage to a world through taking the tiller with a full response, to then, miraculously, co-evolve (manifest) its future destination? Nature is mysteriously transforming as you take sail (become an evolutionary pathway) with the tides and winds of an instinctual awareness and desire to see, be, and become expressive of *who you truly are.*

Chapter II
Story-Mirror Jacqueline Baldet

Jacqueline Baldet explained: "My work is invisible"—yet the difference she has made to many children is what makes it apparent. She is like a creature in the wild whose labor is also invisible. The wholeness and the beauty of Nature, however, is a mirrored reflection of many organisms who weave her patterns in their unique ways. The subtext to Jacqueline's personal history includes the unexpected effects of a human response to the same transcendent patterns. She believed that we enter the world with an impulse and attraction to express these in personal ways.

"We are each born with a unique capability and if we do not discover what it is, or cannot fulfill its potential, it will become our ultimate frustration." This is a medium or type of work that could express one's own universal self-expression. Its engagement is how we weave with Nature, also supremely important to us personally. We want to be seen and heard for a much bigger coevolutionary human work which – if you are not Jacqueline – has remained a mystery. She would occasionally announce: "I give children better than everything. I don't take anything away." She meant the impulse and attraction that we come into the world with. She referred to it as our golden thread calling but it is the same as the desire-prompted / process-based universal self-impulse and attraction. She knew that following the thread would organically reveal a personal relationship with the cosmos.

Jacqueline never doubted guidance from her instincts and heart and therefore her life shows what is possible when a human and universal purpose combine. She departed from the earthly plain in March 2019. We met when she was the governess to my three younger siblings in the early 1960s and we stayed in touch since then. She told me a story about my brother Wade, an example of her invisible labor of love that made all the difference in the world for him.

We lived in Lakeville, Connecticut, about two hours by car from New York City. It was Jacqueline's birthday and she was scheduled to leave for the city to join friends who had planned a special evening. She made it clear to Wade and my sister Alexandra that they had to complete their homework by 4:00. Wade, who was nine at the time, saw this as an opportunity to manipulate Jacqueline by ignoring her request. She did not see this as disobedience. Rather, his choice to manipulate was a direct threat to his golden thread getting taken away—by the force of his separated behavior.

Wade greatly admired our grandfather, Louis Marx, who was known as the "Toy King" as he was a pioneer in mass production in the 1950s and '60s. Granddaddy had a big heart, which one would expect of someone who makes toys, but he was also motivated by materialistic goals to be rich, famous, and powerful. When he died, he left a large portion of his fortune to the Boy Scouts, which showed his generosity, yet he died a lonely man. His motto was "*do your best and be **the** best*"—geared toward achieving physical goals.

At nine years old Wade wanted to be like him, when he saw how successful a bombastic approach could be. He might have been less tempted if his golden thread and unique capability for music had been seen by our parents.

Wade's first guitar was a flimsy plastic toy that did not tune properly. One day his frustration got the better of him and he threw and broke it on the ground. He asked Dad for a new and "good" guitar but our father refused, believing Wade had acted irresponsibly. Jacqueline intervened when she intuited the problem. Her solution was to purchase a well-made guitar with her own money, which he had to repay with his weekly allowance. Her real objective was to not reinforce his bombastic separated self, while at the same time she was supporting him in getting a hold on his golden thread.

At 3:30 Jacqueline was dressed and ready to go to New York, but Wade had not budged on his homework. Her invisible work suddenly became apparent when she decided to stay home. It was too good an opportunity for her to take a stand for what was whole about him. Without words she brought him a message of love, silently expressed: he did not have to be more than he is.

Jacqueline had a golden thread—universal self-education. Its focus compares with the Latin derivative of educate, *educare*. It means to *lead forth* or to *draw out*. The best thing she gave children was to not take away the deeper meaning of their life; in the case of a golden thread calling, it is a coevolutionary relationship with the cosmos. Responding cellularly and emotionally draws out an animated and animating experience of a connection with the larger whole. People describe the unveiling and experience of this—their Pearl Beyond Price or Holy Grail. This proves the highly spiritual way humans respond to their relationship with Nature. Another subtext to Jacqueline's history paints a picture of the non-local, coevolutionary effects of choosing to follow her thread. Non-locality describes the intimate connection which exists between the physical world and its underlying fabric, the invisible quantum universe.

A friend once asked her how she knew so much when her formal education had ended at age 13. She replied that everything she knows "comes from the Wisdom of the Unwritten Book of Life." Following her golden thread drew out its consciousness and its unitive perspective prompted aligned choices at every turn in the road. She stayed on track and never let go of its textured filament. The Pearl Beyond Price, for Jacqueline, was when following her thread was how her life miraculously took care of itself. This is a highly unusual (non-local) experience, for anyone who views themselves as separate.

Jacqueline was born in 1924 in the French town of Auch, where her parents owned a successful gourmet food and wine business. They lost everything when the Great Depression hit. She had just graduated from the equivalent of middle school at the very young age of 13, but her parents could not afford a higher education. Her response was typical of someone whose golden thread had not been taken away. If she was not going to school, then she would work instead. With an unyielding confidence, she marched to the shed behind her house and got her bike, then looked out over the horizon. In the distance were the smokestacks for the glove factory, *Jonquet Pere et Fils*. With no delay, she hopped on her bike and made a beeline to possible employment, with no concern for being underage. This problem miraculously took care of itself when she was hired, and by eighteen Jacqueline was financially independent.

In 1956 she emigrated to the United States by way of Canada. Jacqueline had been living in Canada with her sister and brother-in-law, when the couple decided to emigrate to the U.S. She liked the idea too, but her paperwork was incomplete. There would not be enough time to retrieve the missing information, before the U.S. border was to close for two years. Bureaucratic red tape was not going to get in Jacqueline's way, however. She requested an interview with the U.S. consulate, with the same confidence about crossing political borders that she'd shown earlier in not allowing being underage to block her progress.

The day of her interview, she saw a substitute consul who was none other than Nobel laureate Pearl S. Buck. She spoke with Jacqueline for an hour and a half and was very moved by her life's story. At the end, she took Jacqueline's hand tenderly in hers and said, "You carry a message that my country has lost a long time ago. It is a message of love." This was the message she brought to Wade—not verbally, but with her invisible work of drawing out and mirroring his true self. Imagine some of the consequences of a universal self-education. Why wouldn't the effect of your life taking care of itself, for example, be how to offset demands for external sources of energy?

Inventor Saul Griffith is skeptical that the world could make the transition to non-carbon-based and renewable energy systems in time before atmospheric temperatures reach dangerously high levels. Even if it were possible, the amount of energy generated from these systems may not be enough to keep up with current demands. Based on calculations he made in 2010, the average rate of global consumption of energy is: "... *sixteen trillion watts or terawatts*"—the equivalent of *"a hundred and sixty billion hundred-watt light bulbs burning all the time."*[9]

In order to replace all but three of the sixteen terawatts, using renewable energy systems in the time frame necessary, it would require the construction of

> ...a hundred square meters of new solar cells, fifty square meters of new solar-thermal reflectors, and one Olympic swimming pool's volume of genetically engineered algae (for biofuels) every second for the next twenty-five years; one three-hundred-foot-diameter wind turbine every five minutes; one three-gigawatt nuclear power plant every week... Understanding energy better is only part of the solution. Griffith believes... We've been working on energy, as a society, for a few thousand years, so we've already turned over most of the stones... Wrestling with human nature...[10]

...has to be part of the plan.

Jacqueline did wrestle with the separated wounded parts of children, which most of us struggle with as adults. Before we are taught what to think and do in life, we are naturally attracted to discovering our golden thread coevolutionary calling. When various types

---

9   David Owen, "Annals of Design, The Inventor's Dilemma: An eco-minded engineer discovers the limits of innovation," *The New Yorker Magazine,* May 17, 2010, 42.
10 Ibid., 50.

of education replace responding, we become fractured and a disorientation begins. It is easy to lose the thread of our true self; we are then at risk of losing the world that sustains us, when we exploit it externally. If an evolutionary map could show where we are in its big history, the coronavirus has brought us to the point where we risk losing the world—our civilization. Jacqueline was aware of the critical aspect of acknowledging the trauma *and* supporting finding the golden thread and following its direction. The invisible work of becoming integrated is what renews the world as we gently wrestle and heal the alien separated self. Responding to what our instincts and emotions know about our true identity, reliably expresses intimacy, compassion, and great humility when no separation is seen. Not only does this express a message of love and the unitive wisdom of the unwritten book. Its attractive force, at this historical moment, could guide and initiate global and planetary healing simply by acknowledging what is whole in each and all of us. This could set the foundation for a world that would work equally well for everyone.

~ Your LifeBook Journal

The way Jacqueline related multi-perceptually added up to a life that was full of miracles, adventure, and expressed personal freedom. It testifies to a quality of existence, when relating this way is how to develop a coevolutionary relationship with the cosmos. She met her needs non-locally when they were offset by Nature's law of mutual sustainability. The story about Wade provides solid gold coevolutionary tips. She knew if you want to follow your golden thread, it also requires healing the wounded separated self. Can you imagine becoming Jacqueline, who does this for yourself? Her advice was always: never let go of your thread, and think with your heart. The details will reliably sort themselves out.

Chapter III
Story-Mirror The Snowstorm

Winter of 2011, the Washington, D.C., area was hit by two massive snowstorms, occurring within a very short period of each other. My husband Sandy and I were living in Takoma Park, Maryland, which borders the District of Columbia. Most side streets were semi-passable after the first storm but when the second one descended, everything came to a complete halt. The business-as-usual world could not keep going under three-plus feet of snow. The void created was an opportunity for something else to replace the divided world of politics, itself a mirrored reflection of long-held beliefs: all in life is separate. From that common standpoint, it is wise to prioritize looking out for your own self-interest. Yet as street signs and curbs all disappeared under sheeting veils of snow, so too did layers upon layers of separate identities lift from the neighbors. Underneath the weight of the weather emerged a sensation of being one and living in the same world. In the pure whiteness of the snow a bond formed in the neighborhood, transcending ideologies and moving us into the alternative universe (for us)—one that thrives with interdependent relationships.

Neighbors flocked into the snow-covered streets like birds preparing for a great migration. The Latin derivative for migrate is *migrare*, akin to the Greek word *ameibein*, which means change—these described the nature of the snowy journey. The changes that took place in my neighborhood reflected a shift from the *normal* separated identities of class, race, and gender to one mirroring a shared natural experience. It was not a visible connection as much as it was a rhythm of life: the more in step we became, the further we migrated or changed from linear focuses to snowy-blowy transcendent self-experiences.

As night fell I looked outside my window at the wisteria vine tangling its way across the front of my porch. Nine mourning doves were taking refuge from the storm all huddled together with no concern for my presence. In the silence of the void of the business-as-usual world, constantly clamoring for power and control, an alternative world unfolded based on trust. This can happen when Nature steps forward, as she did with the snowstorm, and becomes the world – whether you are human or a dove – where all is one. Superficial differences separating one person or species disappeared in the cyclonic rhythm of a winter snowstorm.

The subtext to the Snowstorm story is an evolutionary tale when a shared sense of identity restores trust and replaces objectives for power and control with a new tendency to collaborate and coevolve. There is a natural rhythm of give-and-take whose experience organically inspires intimate relationships and a desire to support mutual sustainability. An alternative to the separate world could emerge – immediately – anywhere people are being uplifted by a sense and desire for connection.

The next day the sun was extra brilliant and the everyday beauty of Nature replaced the routine frustrations of modern life. The snowy world sparkled through ice-prisms—and as it refracted rainbow colors in the air, also melted on my cheeks and tingled its beauty through the language of sensation.

The sensuousness of the natural world became a joyful experience of being alive. Many people were without electricity, others did not have shovels sturdy enough to handle three feet of snow, and a few were physically disabled and therefore could not consider attempting such a demanding exercise. However, the effect of a multi-sensory experience was it expanded the horizon of the meaning of being human and alive. This was life-changing, and we migrated in the direction of living interdependently. This was a big departure from the usual separated view, which believes you must deal with your problems alone.

Nobody dared cast snow into the streets; it would then have been more difficult for the snowplows to pass. Nor did anyone dispose their loads onto other people's yards, possibly crushing a buried shrub. Instead, people worked together and distributed shoveled snow strategically around neighbors' plants so that when it melted, the water would replenish the moisture lost during the long summer droughts. The new rhythm of giving and receiving orchestrated this intuitive and love-guided process.

We found our balance with a natural rhythm the more responsive we became to one another and the snowy world around us. In the process of addressing an emergency, we were also weaving new patterns connecting work, play, and spirituality into one integrated way of life. Without traveling any distance, a change from fragmented existences to one that was seamlessly inclusive became our world. You may believe no new frontiers remain to be discovered on Earth but an entire other world exists, waiting to be imagined with integrated multi-perceptual awareness. This is because seeing and being inclusive allows Nature to expand with human connectivity. What could unfold in the wake of a pandemic, for example, might address its emergency; relying on integrated understanding could also manifest human expressions of her sacred unity. Cultivating symbiotic relationships could lead to experiencing *real support from the elements of Nature.*

As I was digging endlessly, I saw a possibility for myself, as if the new rhythm inspired its realization. My weaving studio was in a dark, damp, and cold basement—a mirrored reflection of the low level of appreciation for this type of work in a high-powered political town. This impression had caused me to develop a wounded separated self. The opportunity to step out of a painful environment renewed a sense of a more universal significance of my work. It is my animated (golden thread) expression of life being me weaving and coevolving. My artistic process has the same coevolutionary give-and-take rhythm as digging snow, when both are invisible labors of love. This type of purpose cultivates symbiotic relationships with the surrounding world. I suddenly felt ready to take a leap of faith and trust this problem would take care of itself when its elemental impulse would naturally elicit help from a coevolutionary cosmos.

The physical appearance of our species has not altered much over the past 200,000+ years. However, our ability for conscious awareness has radically transformed the environment and the realities we live in. The force behind its evolution is the *meme*. In 1976 evolutionary biologist Richard Dawkins, in his book *The Selfish Gene*, introduces the *meme*—thoughts. Ideas, concepts, and beliefs are memes and according to Dawkins, have influenced human evolution even more than genetic mutations such as those responsible for walking upright, our opposing thumbs, and large brain. The important thing to understand about memes, which mirror primarily a rational process of understanding, is they have the power to become realities.

The neocortex part of our brain is where thoughts propagate but they become new realities when an idea is "imitated" by followers. Religion, hierarchical systems, and an economic purpose are replacements for responsive coevolutionary living. Dawkins describes how we got to where we are today.

> [memes are] achieving evolutionary change at a rate that leaves the old gene panting far behind...Memes propagate themselves in the meme pool by leaping from brain to brain via a process which, in the broad sense, can be called imitation.[11]

The Snowstorm was a big interruption in this evolutionary process. It tells the story of what can happen when people find a balance with the natural rhythm of whole-oriented purposes. People in my neighborhood did not choose to develop symbiotic relationships,

---

11 James Gleick, "Have Meme Will Travel: Information Behaves Like Life Itself. And vice versa," *Smithsonian Magazine*, May 2011, 42: 2, 88.

but it proves the potential to do this intentionally. Making a choice in its own right can become a force of change. It was a decision, after all, made by our hunter-and-gatherer ancestors, to no longer identify with Nature and instead to harness her resources to do human work, paving the way to the world we live in. Fulfilling this choice of purpose required developing the rational mind.

Between 13,000-10,000 B.C., Natufian settlements marked a transition from a hunter-and-gatherer lifestyle to more settled social structures. Villages appeared in the area surrounding modern-day Israel, Palestinian territories, Lebanon, Jordan, and western Syria.[12] By 6,000 B.C. the transition from hunter-and-gatherer to agrarian societies was just about complete, especially in the Fertile Crescent area.[13]

A temple in Gobekli Tepe, Turkey, has been discovered—built by hunter-gatherers before agriculture became established, between 9,600-8,200 B.C. Archeologist Klaus Schmidt, who worked at the Heidelberg University in 1994[14] and was part of the German Archeological Institute when he discovered the temple, posits a theory. Its construction may have symbolized an early replacement for instinctual and emotional, life and self-awareness. Schmidt sees a connection.

> The human impulse to gather for sacred rituals arose as humans shifted from seeing themselves as part of the natural world to seeking mastery over it.[15]

Schmidt identifies the memetic replacements for Nature's call. Over the course of 11,000 years, these have diversified from many

---

12 Charles C. Mann, date from "Where Farming Began," *The Birth of Religion* (Supplement), *National Geographic Magazine*, 219:6, 2011.
13 Ibid.
14 Elif Batuman, "The Sanctuary: The World's Oldest Temple and the Dawn of Civilization," *The New Yorker Magazine*, Dept. of Archeology, Dec 19, 2011, 78.
15 Mann, Archeologist Klaus Schmidt's view explained, 57.

different imitations into just as plentiful separate realities. This explains why dominant perspectives to this day polarize. Each expresses a particular bias that affects different people either positively or negatively.

> A shift from animism to centralized religion, and from an egalitarian to a hierarchical society, was the cause and not the effect of economic change.[16]

My next-door neighbor Karl, who I rarely ever saw, took it upon himself to shovel out one of the two sidewalks bordering my corner lot. He barely said anything when I thanked him. It occurred to me that in the same way one does not thank a bird, butterfly, whale, or tree for their invisible work—Karl had found his place in a world of interdependent relationships.

Another neighbor was speaking the same language. I also rarely saw him, but he appeared almost on cue to help me remove snow from a fir tree about to break under the weight. I had been struggling to reach its top with a bamboo pole, but even with the help of a ladder I was coming up short. He immediately offered a hand and with his added height and strength, we liberated it, and celebrated as if it were *our* tree.

I had been distrustful of this neighbor, not based on personal experience but, as it were, *idle* gossip had burdened me with a polarizing impression. The snowstorm not only blew away the business-as-usual world but also cleansed a feeling of separateness. What was left was the simple truth—we are mutually related and mutually defining. The doves in my wisteria had also come under the spell of a shared universal self-witnessing.

A few years after the snowstorm, my cousin planned to sell her house on Vashon Island in the *other* Washington. The property included a studio with abundant natural light, and the Mother-Tree,

---

16 Batuman, 80.

as I call her, expanding just outside the window. We bought the house and Sandy and I migrated both physically and with personal changes from the hierarchical-material world to one with a renewed sense of purpose. The problem of a damp and dark studio seemed to take care of itself.

At face value the Snowstorm story could be understood as a group of people who were trying to "get back to normal." However, what took place was far from what *is* normal. For a brief moment the worlds of Nature and humans entangled as work, play, and spirituality became one coevolutionary activity. Before its alternative world could materialize, a FedEx truck came careening down the street. The driver showed no regard for a child, adult, pet, or squirrel that could have been walking in the street to avoid the slippery sidewalks. "Time is money" is the old familiar meme driving the business-as-usual world considered by most to be normal.

Nobody wants to go back to the 'normal' before the pandemic struck. The shaky socioeconomic infrastructure collapsed because business as usual is not a labor of love; it does not imagine a shared identity and mutually supportive purpose. A return to basics is a leap forward when trust and faith in a sense that all are interconnected also reestablishes a relationship with Nature. We join a world that evolves as a whole.

~ Your LifeBook Journal

The pre-civilization world of hunters and gatherers was cruel, dark, and ignorant of everything rational thinking has made possible to understand. On the other hand, our primitive ancestors revealed a potential we still have today: to identify with a shared universal identity and act accordingly. Does imagining your primordial tendency have a futuristic flare? Hybrid breeds of plants, when they are left to reseed, will return to their original genus. The Snowstorm story revealed a similar return to baseline human universal self-awareness—before memes created our world. What do you think could happen if you chose to identify with the golden thread of this experience? Do you have a sense of your coevolutionary destiny?

Chapter IV
Story-Mirror Peter and Renée

To teach aerobic dance at a community college you need a higher education, but there is no preparedness required to become a parent and raise a child. When my son Peter was born, I did not know what to expect but quickly realized how complex a human being is. This is due to the impulses and attractions, which are of critical importance to us personally, but their purpose and the world they relate to are unknowns that take us to the edge of what is possible to imagine.

Jacqueline Baldet was an early explorer of our mystery and she identified important clues such as our relationship with the cosmos. We discover what our connection is by responding to the golden thread of our primary personal impulses and attractions.

This chapter's story-mirror refines understanding with identifying a golden thread calling. I describe the challenges of protecting its unifying potential, while schools aim to develop rational skills for living separately. I was fortunate enough to be able to follow my children as they followed their golden threads.

One of my main objectives was for them to avoid developing a separated self. I listened with love and curiosity in between what my instincts and heart were sensing and feeling and how I could think to honor the deeper meaning of their lives. At the same time, I had to ensure they could manage in the world as it is—albeit in need of a radical transformation.

Peter arrived in 1977 and when he was a toddler it became clear something more than a childish whim was attracting him. Sometimes it seemed like he was rummaging through a haystack of the usual concerns about children, which when enforced, only piled more straw on the heap that he had to dig through. He was searching for the needle and golden thread of his life with which he would sew an invisible seam between his personal and universal purpose.

The challenge for me was trusting that his instincts and emotions would provide the path to his full development, which conflicted with pedagogical concerns whether he was right brained, left brained, an audio, visual, or kinesthetic learner. His curiosity would eventually inspire a whole-brain or multi-perceptual awareness when a desire to know the meaning of cellular and emotional feedback engages all the different ways humans relate.

I struggled with navigating educational choices which, even if they take an alternative approach to competition-driven learning, still are required to meet the same academic standards as mainstream educations, in order to become accredited.

I enrolled Pete in a Montessori pre-school program where he continued through the second grade. I appreciated founder Marie Montessori's view of *follow the child*. It reminded me of Jacqueline's universal self-guided education. Unfortunately, children are followed up to a point and then no further. We might find the needle and golden thread in the haystack, but it will be used to sew along the bottom line of the materialistic objectives of the Anthropocene. I discovered creative ways to work around this problem, however.

At the end of the second grade it became clear, Pete had become disoriented by what he was learning at school; it distracted him from catching hold of his golden thread and unique capability. One day I happened to meet his kindergarten and second-grade teachers in the parking lot, and his second-grade teacher jokingly said, "I don't think Pete could spell 'cat' if he tried." His reputation of being distracted had become endearing! I was stunned.

The Unwritten Book

I had to look for other options more like an explorer than a mother who was trying to find an educational environment which could develop his unique capability, rather than become his ultimate frustration, were this to remain undiscovered and unskilled. My choices were limited. Academic educations replace rather than expect the golden threads of an evolutionary consciousness which mirrors the wisdom of the heart. I took on an explorer's attitude with having to decide: was I going to sail the uncharted seas of existing educations or bushwhack through a pathless jungle of academic requirements? Discovered by sea or in the jungle, I was looking for "one thing" related to his golden thread so that he could catch hold.

I personally liked the Montessori experiential and collaborative approach to learning. Pete, however, was more interested in knowing why what he was learning was important. This was a clue to the universal quality of his calling. His golden thread related to something being expressed in his school subjects. Perhaps his impulse and attraction sensed and felt something priceless or eternal was being communicated through them. He needed to know why math, literature, history, and art mattered.

I took this to mean he needed a more academic learning environment and enrolled him in an all-boy Catholic school. The institution made a point of students becoming aware why each subject was important by the many tests and papers they were expected to accomplish. He thrived and became a very good student. He would gleefully ask me to "quiz him" on a subject that he felt proud about knowing so much. The experience stabilized him, and he could freely enter a new personal cycle of imagining beyond the goals of his academic education.

When Pete was about nine years old, he *curated* his own museum. It was situated in the foyer, underneath a large staircase. He collected household items, such as china that I used for special occasions, as well as rocks, seashells, sea-glass, and driftwood, which he had collected during family reunions at the seashore in California. His exhibit also included age-worn hand tools and hand-me-down kitchen utensils. These were "priceless" because they held memories of family gatherings and relationships. Pricelessness is a quality of experience that transcends the finite and material. It became Pete's inner compass which guided his steps. He never let go of this golden thread, and his life became a gesture of honoring it.

His impulse and attraction led him to book publishing, his unique capability, where he acquires and edits non-fiction. He weaves the strands of historical threads with strings of literature and philosophy into fabrics of priceless stories.

Peter and Renée are twelve years apart and when she was born, I had developed an evolutionary perspective that made her response to her impulse and attraction seem less complex. I expected her coevolutionary gift, like a Buddhist anticipates this contribution with each reincarnation of the Dalai Lama. This, however, did not make it easier to support her with following its lead. Unlike Pete's golden thread, which became activated with a traditional education, Renée was completely off the grid. She skipped the rummaging through the haystack phase and was immediately in synch with her universal awareness. In fact, what she instinctively knew, reminded me of a major revelation a person might arrive at from a life of dedicated meditation. She innately understood the relationship between the one-whole and the many different physical expressions. She could morph into a cloud, a flock of geese, a deer, the sound of rain on my garden bucket, and sometimes she was a little girl. Her favorite game was to get into a box and pretend she was being delivered by UPS. I would open it up and swoon at the adorable little deer, which just arrived.

Her identity was fluid and it neutralized the boundaries that separated fields of thought in anthropology, philosophy, and art. They were the history of conscious awareness of the oneness of life, as seen through their different lenses. After many cycles of following her thread, it guided her to take these subjects, which she considered to be one and the same. She may have not gotten to this point, if assessments of her intelligence as a young child had become a wounded separated self—and if she identified with it, this would have taken away her golden thread.

She came into the world with an already developed multi-perceptual awareness. The problem is, this is not the skill that children are tested for. Every child is *special* until they enter first grade. When she was a kindergartner, her class was asked to describe what each child thought was special about them. They made drawings and collages depicting a wide range of specialness. Some had a unique talent or a brother or sister who meant a lot to them. Interestingly enough, Renée wrote in her wavy scrawl "I love school," which was ironic. She took the mandatory standardized "school readiness test," and Sandy and I were told that she tested as a "slow learner." The suggestion was she take remedial skill-building classes, especially in math and critical thinking. These subjects develop rational skills, ones Renée did not have as a first grader.

She loved the Greek myths, poetry, and art, and to think of her stuck in classes with no meaning other than to practice drill after drill, would have surely taken her golden thread away. We transferred her to a combination Montessori-Waldorf school. We loved its approach and she did too, but through no fault of its own, it had to prepare children to enter the same competition-driven world as mainstream educations. Society has low expectations of children who are not motivated by competition and this can influence a teacher's view, even in a school that does not advocate it. One of Renée's teachers told me, meaning it to be a compliment, "Renée is a wonderful person, and heaven knows we need more people like her in the world, but she will never be a leader."

I decided to homeschool Renée as I knew competition-driven leadership is just the sort of human activity that needs transforming when its individualistic goals have become unsustainable. This has become even more apparent during a pandemic—world leaders, instead of mounting a coordinated effort to fight the virus, are blaming, competing, and excluding one another. I used the Calvert homeschool curriculum as a roadmap, but we veered down many side roads with artistic, philosophical, and anthropological conversations.

We blended these into one woven tapestry of thought in order to appreciate a world connected through a synthesis of these different perspectives—the one and the many are essentially the same.

We homeschooled for six years and when she graduated from "Mom's School" after completing the 7th grade, because we focused on quality and not quantity, she entered high school and moved on to college and graduate schools. She has since meandered like a river – just like she used to morph into one as a little girl – through her favorite subjects. Renée has found a natural rhythm and cycle by following her thread of ongoing awareness of the oneness of life, and in the process – at least for the time being – she loves school.

Peter was rationally inclined as a child but as an adult he has developed a passion for painting. Renée, on the other hand, entered the world creative, but her golden thread to express what she saw multi-perceptually, guided her into a life of scholarship. Following your impulse and attraction, therefore, is both a creative and intellectual process. It requires integrating a whole mind, body, heart awareness—evolving in its own time with cycles and seasons of following the golden thread.

Archeologist Klaus Schmidt, like evolutionary biologist Richard Dawkins, understood the power of the mind and consciousness to manifest like realities. The world we experience is an effect of a pre-dawn choice to no longer identify with Nature, which developed the rational mind. Schmidt muses on the fountainhead of the existing civilization, while I am imagining an ecologically-based civilization that emerges from an integrated multi-perceptual mind. A choice to identify with and respond to the deeper thread of our life is what orchestrates its potential.

> Twenty years ago everyone believed civilization was driven by ecological forces…I think what we are learning is that civilization is a product of the human mind.[17]

---

17 Klaus Schmidt, cited in Mann, "The World's First Temple," *The Birth of Religion* (Supplement), *National Geographic Magazine*, 219:6, 2011, 58.

When my goal for raising my children has been to protect their source of inner guidance, I was careful to never impose my views and personal understanding of the meaning of their golden threads. My story about my children reflects the great mystery which we all share. Our lives are meaningful, but not according to world standards. Instead, it becomes apparent with each personal universal self-expression which could be mirrored by what is priceless or when we sense and feel we are all mutually related and mutually defining.

~ Your LifeBook Journal

Does the image of your golden thread for the sake of the good of the world appeal? Seeing and hearing each other – for the unique coevolutionary story that it weaves – is reassuring and hopeful in 2021 and beyond. We could use a new, adventuresome possibility, unrestrained by a virus. The challenge we face is trusting underutilized aspects of our humanity. We come into the world passionately seeking to cultivate our relationship with a participatory cosmos, but there are no educations that focus on developing multi-perceptual awareness. Can you see yourself as a child in this story-mirror? Do you shimmer with the memory of your golden thread? It is yours to weave a bridge from the failing world of the separated mind to the creative and empathetically orchestrated universe of interdependent relationships.

Part Two

Conscious Evolutionary Perspective

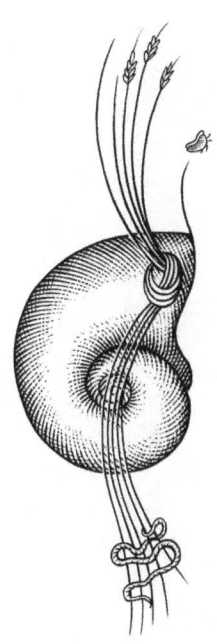

Chapter V
The Evolutionary Crossroads

We might see political disarray, extreme weather events, corruption, and blatant callousness toward the living but underlying are the unseen patterns of chaos of a mass extinction. These are the forces behind a major *evolutionary crossroads*—humans have not only influenced its development but also play a role in determining what kind of world awaits on the other side. In other words, we too are an unseen evolutionary determiner of the future. According to theorist Ervin Laszlo, a "decision" to change how we live is critical to ushering in a mutually sustainable world through what is called a *chaos window*.

There is another unseen "player" in chaos called *a strange or chaotic attractor*. It serves as Nature's feelers for patterns to pave the way to a new planetary cycle. There are two possible directions, and both hinge on a decision about what our human purpose is. One set of patterns could be a continuation of existing separated and independent lifestyles. It is possible to observe this trend in response to the destructive effects of the coronavirus. Many people express the desire to get back to business as usual. If "going back" becomes the attractive force, then it could take us into the devolutionary age of the Anthropocene. There are many, however, who do not think this a good idea. A graffiti artist in Hong Kong, during the first month of the virus' surge, for example, painted on a wall: "We can't return to normal because the normal that we had was precisely the problem."

The other direction could support innate whole-oriented tendencies that express universal self-awareness. COVID-19 could be a physical manifestation of a chaos window. We stand at the threshold of a *super chaos window,* therefore, from compounding effects of both separated thinking and a rogue pathogen. Evidently, according to Laszlo, even a conscious decision to respond – before getting started with the process – could be enough to invisibly or non-locally *breakthrough to a new structure and a new mode of operation.* It could, for example, *chaotically attract* the *age of human conscious coevolution.* Developing an evolutionary perspective is to enable one to identify universal self-impulses and attractions to be "what it is" to make a decision about. Without this reflective view, it is highly unlikely we will choose to take seriously the experiences, which remain mysterious.

A scientific outlook, such as chaos theory, is invaluable when it shows that a decision to become expressive of who we truly are could make all the difference in the world. A conscious evolutionary decision to become reconciled with instinctual universal self-awareness, could at least get us through the door or a chaos window-of-opportunity, to have a say in what type of future it will be. You won't be able to see it, but a love-guided response could affect the quantum ground, in such a way as to be in our favor. It could, for example, *"blow up" to change existing trends and bring new trends and processes into existence.* Even if we cannot *fully* respond to a golden thread calling, the energy of a decision could create a *tiny fluctuation*—then releasing a cascade of radical transformations.

Ervin Laszlo has a hopeful message in a period of upheaval, outlined below. He is very clear about a choice to live differently, which would organically take place when relating multi-perceptually, rather than rationally—a main reason why we hover at the threshold of a major evolutionary crossroads.

> Chaos in modern systems theory defines the state of a system in which its stable cycles and processes give way to complex, seemingly unordered behavior, governed by so-called strange or chaotic attractors. In this state, the system

is responsive even to tiny, sometimes immeasurably small fluctuations.[18]

A chaos-window – in the human-context "decision-window" – is a trajectory period in the evolution of a system during which any input or influence, however small, can "blow up" to change existing trends and bring new trends and processes into existence.[19]

A chaos-point, in turn, is the crucial tipping point in the evolution of a system in which trends that have brought the system to its present state break down and it can no longer return to its prior states and modes of behavior: It is launched irreversibly on a new trajectory that leads either to breakdown or to breakthrough to a new structure and a new mode of operation.[20]

We came into the world with a golden thread calling and unique capability, which is fortuitous: a choice to never let go of it could thread us safely through the eye of a chaos window. Our species getting past its maw, is traversed as one person after another decides to respond to instinctual and emotional feedback on the *other* whole-oriented, coevolutionary human purpose. It could *organically* guide a personal conscious evolution, which might invisibly swap a physical Armageddon for the alternative open-ended future. Relating with an integrated mind, body, heart synthesis – impossible without undergoing healing of personal trauma of separation – has an energetic quality or vibration that may *appeal* to Nature. It could utter the magic tone, whose musicality liberates a

---

18 Ervin Laszlo, *Chaos Point 2012 and Beyond: Our Choices between Global Disaster and a Sustainable Planet* (Charlottesville, VA: Hampton Roads Publishing, 2006), vii.
19 Ibid.
20 Ibid.

sustainable future from the womb of the quantum ground, with its harmonic (tiny) fluctuation.

A silky skein, composed of many people's golden threads, can knot together into a bundled cord of hope. Its hank – a lifeline and human bridge of multi-perceptual awareness – may be a potential that Nature gave us in order to save ourselves. The journey begins with a decision to trust and have faith in our own deepest impulse and attraction, which could invisibly pave the way.

~ Your LifeBook Journal

If there were ever a time to react to our instincts and emotions, it would be now. Chaos is invisible to the eye but is warning us on a cellular level to adapt to new ways of being and living in order to survive. At the same time, however, a decision to respond to any out-of-the-ordinary universal self-impulse and attraction could trigger a *breakthrough to a new structure and a new mode of operation*. Chaos theory is an important perspective when it shows that not only our unconscious lives affect evolution. What we choose or do not choose to respond to, in regard to our unique coevolutionary relationship with Nature, has reached a boiling point in the history of our planetary system. Separated thinking and lifestyles, which correspond with the many disconnections, may have paved the way to a chaos window. Now that we are here, there is also a window of opportunity to have a say in the direction that Nature will take. We have entered Part Two, through the portal of a chaos window. Light is seen at the end of a dark tunnel with a multi-perceptual responsiveness to instinctual and emotional feedback. Illuminated is the path of a conscious evolutionary decision. It is the way of compassionate healing of personal trauma and also passionately expanding by choosing to never let go of the golden thread. This is a practical understanding of a universal self-guided, conscious evolutionary perspective and process. Can you sense and feel our species' role in the influencing of a planetary collapse? On the other hand, do you also have an intuition that a decision to go the whole way, responding to your life's great attraction, is where the solutions lie?

Chapter VI
Conscious Evolution

The perspective of conscious evolution came from my parents, Barbara Marx Hubbard and Earl Wade Hubbard. It was a way for them to map the history of the evolution of ideas. They agreed with Richard Dawkins who viewed this human potential to be more significant to our development than genetic mutations. However, my mother firmly believed it is necessary to choose peaceful purposes for ideas, such as alternatives to the creation of weapons of mass destruction. Making this choice, therefore, guides a conscious evolution of such powerful capabilities.

My parents also came to the conclusion the world is at an evolutionary tipping point. They understood the evolution of consciousness having reached a critical mass, which has transformed into a human-driven force of creation. They considered the Apollo Space program in the 1960s, which enabled humans to leave Earth's atmosphere, a sign of the transcendent and transformational potentials for ideas, such as those that made space travel possible. In fact, my father went a step further. The evolution of consciousness has become a human *Creative Intention*. My mother, on the other hand, viewed the sum of cultural achievements as having developed into a noosphere or collective mind-sphere. My parents were visionaries who had the courage to express their golden thread callings. May we too be able to do the same, when each thread is a decision the future will expand with what is whole and good rather than diminish to become a sub-human existence. It is never known exactly how each unique thread weaves into a future fabric because the sum of all the input will be the telling truth.

Barbara and Earl met in 1949 in Paris at Chez Rosalie, a little restaurant on the Left Bank. There was open seating at a long table and two empty stools opposite each other remained as if it was destined that they would meet. Without hesitating my mother asked my father her two very big questions, which she asked of everybody. "What is the purpose of Western civilization?" and "What is the purpose of our advanced powers that could serve a greater good?" She was responding to the recent dropping of the bombs on Japan.

Her question dovetailed with my father's artist's statement: "I am an artist. I wish to find a new image of humanity that is commensurate with our new powers with which to shape the future."[21]

My mother's view of the meaning of Western civilization was inspired by the perspective of French philosopher and Jesuit priest Pierre Teilhard de Chardin (1922). He imagined a noosphere or mind-sphere created from the evolution of ideas and culture. She considered the noosphere a signal that a new awakened age of conscious evolution has begun. This predates but also presages the Internet. A mind-sphere is shared by all. My mother hopefully envisioned a planetary awakening through the collective eyes of the noosphere.

My father called the image of cultural achievements the Creative Intention, which replaces Nature's process. Ideas have transcended the physical bodies of thinkers and have reached the density of a supernova star. The Creative Intention triggers the explosion of a cultural star and its fragments will seed a new universe of ideas. While growing up, my siblings and I were being prepared to go into space in search of new images to reflect on and new worlds imprinted by new ideas. This is a quote from my mother in the newspaper *The State*, in South Carolina, in 1970.

---

21 Barbara M. Hubbard, *Conscious Evolution: Awakening the Power of our Social Potential* (Novato, CA: New World Library, 1998), 23-24.

The Hubbards settled in Connecticut, raised five children, and began their search for a new image of man. Their three daughters and two sons, ranging in age from eight to nineteen, are avid followers of their parents' dream.

"The possibility of new worlds has given new hope for us to indicate to our children," Mrs. Hubbard said. "It has given us a great hand in discipline, because we know we have a new criterion in excellence to challenge them with. We tell them they have to be superior in every way if they anticipate going to other planets. They are zealous missionaries."

Of course, this was wishful thinking, but it indicates how deeply they believed in their vision of the future of conscious evolution—of a universal humanity. Fifty years since this article was written, our species and the planetary system have arrived at a threshold of a major evolutionary crossroads—of which the pandemic apocalypse is a visible example. I will present the idea of conscious evolution as it is relevant to my parents' work.

A circle of people has assembled at the doorstep of the crossroads. We are outside, evening shadows are beginning to fall and there is a fire with dancing flames in the middle. Barbara and Earl Hubbard are tonight's visionaries who will present their hopeful ideas on what the sum of conscious awareness has evolved into, which will have an impact on the future. My father will be the first to speak.

Earl:

And what mankind now seeks is another environment of awareness. To reach it, we must leave the earth, and the result of leaving the earth and going to the moon and Mars will be the evolution of a new species… The new species will be, in our awareness, the first cultural species. We are the

Creative Intention and we are now at a stage of self-awareness. We will thus act differently than we have in the past. We have come through a violent past, but at the time we were involved in it, we had no feelings, and therefore could not conceive of it as violent...Through self-awareness, we will be cleansed of violence. The real reason for going to the moon might very well be to shuck off our violent past and find a world in which our cultural capacities can thrive.[22]

Earl:

If we think in terms of levels of consciousness, we could visualize a darkness that rises through gradations of grays to a level of luminous stardust. The level of stardust is the level of prisms and our self rises through these prisms...What does the light of awareness mean? Now, we are turning in on our self, like a collapsing star creating a crucible, and it would appear that we are viewing the conflagration of all our cultural concepts, but like a collapsing star, we, a cultural star, are evolving within this crucible the essential elements for the next universe, the essential elements for the next level of consciousness.[23]

Earl:

Ideas have clearly transcended the body phase. "E equals MC squared" did not pass with the body we call Einstein, nor did the words "We hold these truths to be self-evident" pass with the body we called Thomas Jefferson. Nor did the words "By singleness of purpose, By steadfastness of conduct" pass with the body we called Winston Churchill.

---

22 Earl W. Hubbard, *The Creative Intention* (New York, NY: Interbook, 1974), 128.
23 Ibid., 182-183.

These bodies articulated these ideas. These bodies evolved awareness, a conceptual force made manifest in symbols, images, language, or another form of message.[24]

The campfire is now a mound of glowing embers. Its warm light has taken the shape of a cave in the hole of the evening as it sinks into darkness. This inspires a pre-dawn atmosphere, where all we have is our imagination to glow in the dark of a great unknown. My father sits down, and my mother rises and begins to speak her vision.

Barbara:

A radically new phenomenon has emerged world-wide, but it has not yet been recognized. It is called the 'noosphere' by Teilhard de Chardin, in his famous work *The Phenomenon of Man*. The root of the word is noos, meaning mind. The noosphere is the mind-sphere, the thinking layer of the Earth, the larger social body created by human intelligence. It is composed of all the spiritual, cultural, social, and technological capacities of humanity, seen as one interrelated superorganism. It is formed from our languages, our art and music, our religious and social structures, our constitutions, our communications systems, our microscopes, our telescopes, our cars, planes, rockets, laboratories, and more. Although we inherited the geosphere, the hydrosphere, and the biosphere, we have generated the noosphere.

We as individuals have not changed much physiologically or intellectually in the last 2,000 years, but our larger social body – the noosphere – has become radically empowered. We are now being born into an extended social and scientific capacity that has never before existed on Earth. It is through this collective social body of shared intelligence,

---

24 Ibid., 57.

capacities, and systems that we go to the moon, map our genes, clone a sheep, and transmit our television images around the world at the speed of light. It is with this body that we co-destroy or co-create. It is into this body the imaginal cells are born—the still-invisible societal butterfly. Conscious evolution has arisen at this precise moment of history because the noosphere has matured and has given humanity powers to affect evolution by choice.[25]

Barbara:

We are the humans who happen to be born as the noosphere connected and is on the verge of a collective awakening through us. We are like cells of an infant who is being born. We are the ones who must consciously handle the fateful transition from one phase of our evolution to the next.[26]

My mother returns to her seat beside my father and as the fire fades, a great silence pervades the space. The spirit of hopefulness lingers in our imaginations. The creative intention of consciousness may become new worlds to live in and it could also morph into a mind-sphere that makes a transformational planetary awakening possible.

~ Your LifeBook Journal

A valuable contribution of my parents was they understood the transformational potentials for consciousness. They had complete faith in Western civilization, through the development of the rational mind, to catalyze opportunities by the sheer force of ideas. The evolutionary crossroads is pre-dawn to an unknown future. However, it is generally understood that it will be affected by consciousness.

---

25 B. Hubbard, *Conscious Evolution*, 15.
26 Ibid., 36.

Therefore, it is a busy intersection of ideas, on what concepts or aspects of consciousness are influencing the future or could guide it in a hopeful direction. It is a season for a spacious and gracious open mind. This allows for great flexibility in evaluating the different views and picking and choosing parts of them and forming hybrid perspectives. For example, taking the concept for conscious evolution, and adapting it to fulfill a coevolutionary potential is very different from my parents' train of thought. Earl and Barbara tracked the history of the evolution of consciousness, which has evolved into something trans- or post-human as well as replaces Nature. Is this the mystery that you have been feeling? Is it the message that you are receiving at the crossroads? Or, do you sense and feel there is much more to understand about being human and universal self-guided? If it was understood, it could feasibly resolve every crisis that has been influenced by its lack. To see this, however, requires weaving the strands of a coevolutionary perspective.

Chapter VII
Organic Conscious Evolution

I grew up in a home where life's big questions were everyday topics of discussion. What is the meaning of life? Or, what is the purpose of powerful technologies, which could serve a greater good? These dinner conversations we chewed along with our meal. The world of ideas, especially those related to conscious evolution, steeped in my imagination. The notion one could choose a whole-oriented purpose especially resonated, when it reminded me of what I experienced in Nature. If Jacqueline had been there, she would have recognized my frequent escapes into the woods, fields, and wetlands, which surrounded my rural Connecticut home, a sign revealing my golden thread.

I loved to wander in search of salamanders, chipmunks, and turtles—not to catch them, but to observe their lives. I was fascinated by how nothing they did appeared random or trivial. They had a force-like intensity and each activity – mating, nesting, surviving, foraging – was carried out with the utmost sense of purpose. No matter how low a creature was on the food-chain, it was living at the edge of its individual as well as its species' potential to survive and contribute to its ecosystem.

In the process of fulfilling its biological lifecycle, an animal is also coevolving its surrounding environment. Their lives have a whole-oriented purpose. Up close Nature's world appears cruel, yet from far away, coevolutionary relationships reveal her unifying tendency. The physical trauma in the fields and forests mirrors the process of becoming reconciled with the invisible patterns of coevolution. Animals in the wild are instinctually responding and they do not appear to have a choice in the matter. And yet, another way to look at this is: by becoming reconciled they each express the larger whole—being them.

What about us? Perhaps Nature is experimenting with a species capable of becoming universal self-conscious and guided. I realized that animals in the wild were answering my mother's big question—what could serve the larger whole. It was not verbalized; rather it was every organism fitting into the same coevolving reality translating its patterns with great diversity. We could respond to our instinctual and emotional impulse and attraction to the same source and therefore interpret the patterns by living the almost infinite ways that universal self-awareness could be expressed. For example, not only is this possible for each individual, the golden thread callings and unique capabilities of everyone further diversify expressions of the patterns. The only difference between us and a responsive salamander is we must choose to react.

Part One showed examples of *what ifs*, which were the effects of unconscious responses. It is a full consent, however, that has agency when intellectually comprehending we are mutually defining and must also reflect corresponding patterns of being and living. Then it becomes possible for Nature to evolve through us. Part Two began with showing that transformations are highly possible when making the decision to respond could affect non-local phenomena such as a strange or chaotic attractor. When there are no coevolutionary human perspectives it becomes necessary to borrow others, which do not have an ecological purpose, but do mirror what is necessary for human compatibility. Mystic Jean-Yves Leloup provides such an example. *The being That Is What It Is* reflects our transcendent universal self. The *I AM that calls us to be…* on the other hand, is the desire-prompted / process-based impulse and attraction. Its (process-based) universal self-understanding serves as guide in discovering what is in need of a personal conscious evolution. Leloup asks a series of questions to put this into perspective.

Do my acts express my word?
Does my word express my thought?
Does my thought express my desire?
Does my desire express my being?
Does my being express the being That Is What It Is (YHWH),
the I AM that calls me to be?[27]

Animals in the wild live at the edge of their species' instinctual impulse to survive and coevolve, while we must choose to respond to both a visceral and emotional experience of the same call. Responding becomes an integrated expression of the larger whole. A seagull, as I indicated earlier, is not separate from her environment when she looks like the wind and the water. Our great mystery is becoming animated by the larger whole, which is multi-perceptually interpreted: the being That Is What It Is, the I AM that calls me to be. For our every gesture to become a mirror, the separated personality self needs to be reconciled with the whole universal self. Doing this would put us at the edge of our own and our species' becoming expressions of what it means to feel love and act on its impulse.

The word *hologram* is composed of the Greek *holo* and *gramma*, which means whole message. A multi-perceptual response to What It Is (that calls) includes a personal conscious evolutionary decision to hold onto the golden thread. Following its lead is how to organically become both a human hologram – a medium – and, the whole message that mirrors a decision to think with the heart and to take a stand for what is whole and unifies. Leloup, again, puts into perspective the effect that this could have. Passion, compassion, intimacy, humility, goodness, truth, beauty—together describe the perfect pitch vibration of love-motivated universal awareness. These express the whole message and human medium with which social and global environments could emulate the sacred unity of Nature.

---

27 Leloup, Jean-Yves, *The Gospel of Mary Magdalene* (Rochester, VT: Inner Traditions, 2002), 58.

Leloup indicates that nothing less than three ingredients of pure love will create harmony in the world. There could be a connection between the harmonics of love and the vibrational patterns of life.

> What does goodness become when separated from light, consciousness, and truth? A softness that is the gateway to hypocrisy and compromise.
> What does truth become when separated from goodness, love, and beauty? A hardness that is the gateway to fanaticism and persecution.
> What does beauty become when separated from truth and goodness?
> Art for art's sake, an aestheticism that is the gateway to a brilliance that clarifies nothing.[28]

The Snowstorm story showed that an alternative reality could emerge, wherever one shifts from a separate to universal identity. A new earth could emerge from the ashes of the old with a choice to relate and respond multi-perceptually. It transcribes a whole integrated response into human ecosystems where life can take hold. We transform into mirrored expressions of what we coevolve, which is as different as butterfly and caterpillar. Join me in the garden with Renée, to prepare for cultivating the multi-perceptual garden of the subconscious, the first of three organic personal conscious evolutions. The butterfly of a possible new earth plumps in the cocoon of a well-tended inner garden. The chores alchemically and organically liberate our butterfly and its corresponding reality as we till, plant, water, weed, prune, harvest, and ritually compost with the rhythm of integration and conscious evolution. Personal and planetary transformation are two sides of the same coin of mutual sustainability when how we live has a direct effect on the world around us. Conversely, our transparent butterflies, with every

---

28 Ibid, 55.

flap of our wings, convey a gesture that in turn mirrors the cosmos being us.

~ Your LifeBook Journal

The love-guided multi-perceptual process is critical to resolving homelessness, reversing the deterioration of human and natural environments. Seeing, being, and becoming a likeness to what is humanly possible to experience and comprehend is a whole message that assures – a reef shark, a child, a person who is homeless, a mother, an artist, a sea turtle, a salamander, along with the rest of the living world – all will benefit rather than become harmed by our activities. When the double punches of chaos window and pandemic portend Nature warning us, it is increasingly apparent (divisive political and economic objectives are not working) that nothing less than our ability to express goodness, truth, and beauty will save us from the devolutionary impacts of separated thinking with its exclusionary tactics. Does rebuilding from the devastation of a pandemic by becoming harmonized seem simplistic? Or, do you sense and feel its message of love will take care of the details, as Jacqueline indicated it could? A choice to become integrated is choosing life over death, rather than to return to the normal reality, which is doomed to fail. Nothing about you and your universal self-guided life could possibly be viewed as trivial ever again!

Part Three

Coevolutionary Perspective

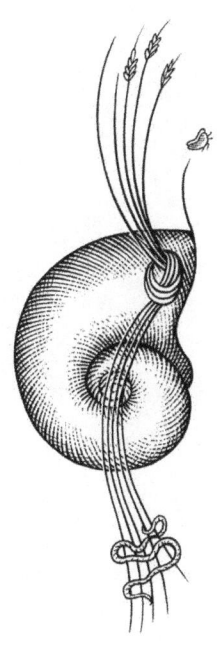

Chapter VIII
The Rhythm of Outer and Inner Gardening

When Sandy and I moved to Vashon, Washington, in 2015, the plot where the vegetable garden was had completely overgrown. Its soil was almost impenetrable with a thick thatch of what I called 'wire-grass' due to its massive root system with high tensile strength. There were weeds, like the feisty salmonberry, bristling with thorns, where no garden glove was a match, and I learned quickly not to touch it. There was also a mysterious 'berm,' a cylindrical narrow rise bordering a deck in back of the house. It too appeared to have once been a garden but resembled the contours of a civilization, silently consumed by wire-grass, thistles, and irreverent weeds.

I pondered an abject lack of sensitivity from the weeds toward gardens, which were producing vegetables and flowers. Mixed in with this reflection was my own experience of weeds: of a separated self presenting with the same type of blindness and insensitivity toward shoots and buds of my golden thread. Although living many years in the Washington, D.C., area was enriching, its highly rationally-minded culture affected me in such a way, I experienced habitat loss, like a creature who was out of her element. Unlike Jacqueline, who always came from the larger picture of her relationship with the cosmos, I suffered like my Vashon gardens from personal weeds. They developed from the constant trauma of not being seen and heard for my invisible work—living, weaving, and writing.

Renée came to visit us the first summer we moved, and together we went to the hardware store where we purchased garden boots and a couple of pickaxes. With these in hand, we tromped down to the vegetable garden and took our position at one end of the approximately 25-yard-long plot. Being suburban greenhorns in wielding pickaxes, it took some doing before our technique posed any threat to the wire-grass. Eventually we became like the other force of Nature counteracting the entropy of suffocating weeds. We remembered the second law of thermodynamics from our home-school days, which described energy moving uphill—and so it was with us, an uphill battle with clearing 13-foot garden rows, one at a time.

Every day – Renée in her boots with pink wild horses printed on them, and me in my Mucks – we liberated two lengths. The typically considered mundane garden activity had the same transcendent experience as digging snow, weaving, and raising children. It had the coevolutionary pulse of Nature's patterns: cycle, recycle, order, and reorder old parts into rehabilitated circuits of energy flow. We were boots on the ground with our handheld pickaxes acting as physical thermodynamic catalysts. We unblocked all that could obstruct a strong energy flow within both the gardeners and the garden soil.

Unlike a city's hot-housed rhythm of the work week and business as usual, working in the garden, in the season of tilling the soil, was labor with a flow. It was not mechanized like an economically fueled human environment, which consumes energy like a steam engine until it runs dry. This explains the shortcomings of a closed energy system, as opposed to Nature's, which is open.

Renée and I experienced slipping into the wide-open thermodynamic and coevolutionary rhythm with daily cycles of turning over the stuck clods of weeded earth. The exposed soil had the aroma of silence. I sensed its fertile stillness like an opportunity to cultivate my seeds of universal self-awareness. Its consciousness is the wisdom of the unwritten book, which weaving tapestries and ideas drew out and also led me forth to Vashon. Getting there was a leap of faith.

Its history began when I announced I was going to bring my studio into the light and weave in a dry and warm environment. Its seed became activated when my cousin Claire let me know that she planned to sell her house on Vashon. I took a leap of faith and told her that Sandy and I were going to buy the house. I didn't ask him, however. I trusted that the right time to apprise him of my choice would come, and it did when he subsequently decided to retire. At the moment of "saying yes" to this choice, I encountered the inertia of my separated wounded self.

As Renée and I cleared the ground of weeds in the vegetable garden, I was aware of sloughing off a bricolage of confusion with not knowing who I was, where I came from—and why I felt like I never fit in—anywhere. My separated self carried the weight of the world that shares a likeness to its visage of fissures. I remembered Jacqueline's coevolutionary instructions. If you want to follow your golden thread, it requires healing the trauma of the separated self.

Nurturing plants while also protecting them from weeds is the secret of a green thumb. However, the love-trifecta with intimacy, compassion, and humility heals experiences of separation as it liberates a leap of faith in my instincts.

A lovely slate walkway appeared, along with a fainting rose bush and wavering peony, as I tilled up the crust of the loaf-shaped flower garden. So too did my waffling and weary golden thread begin to germinate and take root as I cleared the weeds and obstructions from my earthy subconscious.

The traumatic impact of being devalued as a stay-at-home mom and weaver – considered a 'dying art' by many in Washington, D.C. – almost took me under. I saw a similar threat to Renée's well-being when she tested as a slow learner. Putting her into remedial classes without supporting her emerging golden thread would have been a heavy dose of entropy, whose unholy hole she might never have been able to crawl out of.

I protected Renée from her golden thread getting taken away and she comes to my aid by supporting me with inner weeding and pruning. I thought about the years of homeschooling, when she and I approached an education as a means of enhancing her innate understanding. We developed the *no-conflict law*. It compares with a coevolutionary relationship based on an ethic of reciprocity. We could *expect to* receive something of equal value—such as a deadline for a college paper being moved, or my cousin Claire selling her house on Vashon.

~ Your LifeBook Journal

The garden of the subconscious is not fixed in a location like a flower bed. It goes with us and everything we do becomes the opportunity to cultivate its transformational potentials. The meaning of being human and alive is felt and sensed in its soil. You carry within yourself its living and breathing earth. Embedded in it are the seeds to solutions relating to the effects of wire-grass separated thinking. Is it possible to reimagine your life a multi-perceptual gardening process? The chores are inspired by an instinctual and emotional response to the bigger picture of coevolutionary relationships where our golden thread weaves the shared fabric of the larger whole. Is it possible to reclaim your subconscious as a living environment? Its garden not only contains seed insights that reveal your mystery, but also Nature speaks to us from the ground with specific emotional guidance. Surrendering is how to cultivate multi-perceptually inspired intellectual understanding in the process of living its message. This describes the transformational work of conscious evolutionary gardening.

Chapter IX
Conscious Evolutionary Gardening: The Seven Garden Chores

The subconscious is why spontaneous instinctual and emotional universal self-experiences are possible. It filters continuous feedback from the source in the forms of inner guidance as to what is in need of expanding and healing to become expressive of who we truly are. Underlying a golden thread calling or a sense of personal trauma are the desire-prompted responses, which create ecological compatibility.

Our gift to the larger whole is making the decision to take these two experiences to heart. Our subconscious is home to the instincts and emotions, which attune us to our unique (impersonal) relationship with Nature. How we become universal self-guided is complex when our own circumstances are complicated. However, without both disconnected and connected experiences, we cannot know if our actions, words, thoughts, desires, and being are aligned or at odds with our coevolutionary relationship or golden thread calling. Our particular psychological *climate* is not accidental, when it creates the perfect conditions to fulfill its latent potential, one person at a time who chooses to go the whole way. This is how Nature evolves through us, being her transforming the planet—together. It is important to have an intimate reference in order to see what needs expanding and adjusting for the sake of personal, global, and planetary transformation.

In contrast, the legacy of human development with memes, as seen in the current era, is: nobody can agree, and everybody thinks they are right. Enforcing views which lack intimacy leaves the door open to hypocrisy, extremism, and confusion. A response to one's own disconnections and golden thread impulses will activate the thermodynamic pulse of healing and comprehensive expanding.

Unlike a garden plot, the inner garden of the subconscious is a portable patch of ground. It goes wherever we travel. A possible *new earth* could be the manifested expression or crop, as a result of conscious evolutionary labors of love in its psychological mulch. The human soil of our subconscious is *middle territory* between us and the invisible patterns of coevolution. A cycle of inner gardening is universal self-guided, which means, tending the garden composes a set of conscious evolutionary garden chores. Each one is performed by choosing to respond to a desire-prompted intuition: what needs adjusting or expanding in order to follow through with instinctual and emotional feedback from Nature who constantly informs us whether or not we are ecologically in step. A cycle of inner gardening circumnavigates its loop with a thermodynamic force of an uphill / adjusting phase and downhill / expanding impulse, which together form the focuses of a personal conscious evolution. The growing season for inner gardening begins with *tilling* the earth of the subconscious, where seeds to a world of coevolutionary humans have remained silent, dark, and mute. Jean-Yves Leloup captures the non-verbal and integrative aspect of inner gardening—*a meditation that arises from the tilled earth of our silence.*[29]

Similar to the way a creature in the wild relates to the bigger coevolutionary picture in its own backyard and home environment, the same is true for us. Let us begin a cycle of conscious evolutionary

---

29 Leloup, Jean-Yves, *The Gospel of Thomas* (Rochester, VT: Inner Traditions, 2005), ix.

gardening where the chores cultivate a relationship with Nature in the human seedbed of our subconscious.

The Seven Conscious Evolutionary Gardening Chores:

Imagine gathering garden tools, such as a hoe, watering can, weeder, and pruner. These symbolize your toolbox of personal evolutionary and conscious evolutionary perspectives. Every sign of feeling called or if its compelling attraction threatens the separated self, we have the conscious evolutionary hardware for managing the thermodynamic oscillations of a personal coevolutionary growing season. Place them by the plot of your earthy subconscious, probably topped with a thick thatch of wire-grass, which is to be expected. Its world of separated thinking is no match, however, when an emotional impulse to penetrate the surface begins a cycle of conscious evolutionary gardening with inner tilling.

Tilling

Breathe deeply into the silent earth of your subconscious and experience the hidden seed of a personal and human mystery enveloped within its geology. Sense and feel the presence of your own coevolutionary impulse and attraction simmering below the surface of a world of other concerns. Respond with taking up your hoe of an evolutionary perspective and till the wire-grass and create an open space. It has been tooled to penetrate face value understanding with the tempered steel of awareness that there is more to being human and alive, which needs excavating. The subconscious is a communal garden we share with Nature and tilling airs out the portal of the in-between. Cleared away are the thistles and prickers of separated thinking that have been allowed to smother, irreverently, the vibrations of resonant instinctual and emotional universal self-feedback. Smell, taste, touch, feel, and hear the texture of the thread of your golden-seed relationship with the larger whole. Its fiber spins the sinew of a species who can become universal self-conscious and guided. Tilling indicates that a series of new relationships are beginning to form. You are more responsive to your instincts and emotions. However, they are intuited as communicating something beyond the personal when experienced as the mystery of a human partnership with the universe. Thus, tilling opens up a coevolutionary connection with Nature. Greater responsiveness inspires a new relationship with your life's great golden thread attraction. It had been viewed as inconsequential, but now is considered the Pearl Beyond Price. It is also the beginning of a new relationship with yourself, when tilling up the barrier that separated thinking has created, reveals in the vitality of an instinctual impulse, the whole message of a shared universal identity. Richard Dawkins and Ervin Laszlo have shown there is a correlation between what exists in the human world that is relative to how and what is possible to comprehend. Therefore, tilling initiates a new multi-perceptual way of relating, which automatically prompts having to make decisions based on what an integrated mind, and subconscious, body and heart awareness reveal. Becoming multi-perceptually universal self-guided organically gets us into the flow of Nature's cyclic loop of mutual sustainability. For example, Renée and I described our experience, the no-conflict law. A multi-perceptual labor of love in the field of the subconscious is an integrated way of relating. It is also how we thermodynamically destroy (till, weed, prune, compost) and rebuild (plant, water, harvest) a sustainable future, from the complex human soil of daily decisions. This is also to say, we form a new relationship with being human. It / we serve as seedbeds for an alternative whole-oriented purpose to germinate, take root, and bear its love-inspired fruits.

Planting

Planting season begins with a choice to embrace our new relationships. Stay close to the ground and try not to get ahead of your thread. It stems from the natural environment, which envelops us in its living web and calls us to weave its patterns by choosing to respond. Tilling opens up the psychological space, making it possible to sense, feel, and think beyond the tangled wire-grass—a lint-trap of separated thinking. Suddenly our senses and emotions begin to germinate with multi-perceptual awareness. This cultivates a new relationship with a golden thread calling, including both a personal and impersonal appeal. Living it is how we see and hear our self and true identity. It is also a *total acknowledgement* of our right to exist. We are born with an essential contribution to the larger whole, which had been experienced as our great mystery. A golden thread guides multi-perceptually, leading one forth in an ecologically sound direction, thus a gift to Nature. We become planted in the fresh soil of a tilled sense of connection with our surrounding, a dynamic experience. Thus, the chore evokes a sense of joining the great murmurations of other life forms who are surging with the same thermodynamic uphill / downhill phases of Nature's universal self-correcting loop cycles. Inner gardening is in this flow. Planting announces a Springtime for the ages has arrived. Through the cracks of tilled wire-grass and hardpan thinking, a new earth receives the light of a desire-prompted / process-based multi-perceptual response to the world around us. Also seen is the integrated butterfly version of our separated caterpillar. It and the new earth are two sides of the same coin: renewing with a whole human experience, a whole energetic and physical universe and self.

Watering

Grab your watering can out of the evolutionary tool shed with a choice to take a leap of faith. Watering is a decision to cross the line, beyond just asking the question—what if I were to nurture the seeds of a completely unfamiliar coevolutionary / transformational life? The direction is impelled instinctively and emotionally, and thus requires seeing the path blind (without the usual rational understanding). A leap of faith will scoot you off-grid and, like Jacqueline Baldet, will require an unyielding confidence in untried and untested guidance from your subconscious mood swings. When these are understood with a coevolutionary perspective, they are paid attention to. Responding to the golden thread of primal instincts and attractions compose the only guidance there is—how to live a coevolutionary and transformational purpose. "How" is profoundly personal when inner watering is letting go of all shame and judgment, thus supporting resiliency. This conscious step of letting go allows a new relationship with your butterfly version to form. Simultaneous with letting go is deciding to never lose grip of your thread; this not only mirrors a personal metamorphosis into who you truly are, but living your truth could make the biggest difference in the world. A choice to maintain a firm hold is how to stay fully hydrated with the free-flowing water of a love-guided life. Its nourishment could sustain us through periods of unsureness. A multi-perceptual relinquishing of habitual self-criticism – due to the psychological pain from not being seen, heard, understood, nor appreciated at the deeper level – fosters compassion. It becomes possible, therefore, to look with tenderness at the parts of our self that we had refused to see. This is critical to the process of personal metamorphosis and due to how individual decisions directly impact our surrounding, the world also discovers its butterfly. Compassionate inner weeding will protect, like our immune system, identifying what is our true self and what represents the alien separated weedy-self. Trusting and having faith provide great downhill momentum and courage to never let go of the thread, even though it will take you through periods of personal turmoil. The miracle with going the whole way is unexpected opportunities pop up as they did for Jacqueline Baldet. Or, you could also experience the relief when discovering there is no conflict blocking a leap of faith.

William Stafford, in his poem "The Way It Is," captures the spirit of conscious evolutionary watering with a choice to never let go of, nor get ahead of, your (golden) thread.

> There's a thread you follow. It goes among
> things that change. But it doesn't change.
> People wonder about what you are pursuing.
> You have to explain about the thread.
> But it is hard for others to see.

While you hold it you can't get lost.
Tragedies happen; people get hurt
or die; and you suffer and get old.
Nothing you do can stop time's unfolding.
You don't ever let go of the thread.

Weeding

Weeding is the intimate, compassionate, and humble tending to our wounded separated self. This chore is performed by choosing to take a stand for the cultivated intuition about what is whole in us. Tilling, planting, and watering tend the seeds and threads of universal self-awareness. Weeding is a delicate and painful process: identifying where our actions, words, thoughts, desires, and way of being are inconsistent with a newly planted life. Your leap of faith will tumble into the thermodynamic uphill inner healing process through tenderly letting go of wounded behaviors and attitudes. The portable garden of the subconscious is the opportunity to progressively weed from one growing season to the next. Inner gardening is how to see the butterfly pupa in the body of an alien separate identity or caterpillar self. Weeding removes its carapace, constituted from a tangled history of misunderstanding and a lack of being appreciated for your thread and its transformational seeds. The weeding season is the existential crisis of metamorphosis. My brother Wade as an adult experienced the liberating effects of inner weeding. It exposed his butterfly of universal wholeness. He wrote a poem a few months before he succumbed to brain cancer titled "Being Fearless." He acknowledges how seeing the truth made all the difference in the world—to him.

Being fearless is
So relaxing

Things aren't scary
Just sometimes challenging

Suzanne F. Hubbard

When I stop and think it through
There is always a very good answer

Usually from a much bigger picture
Than the small view I had
That's why,

Being fearless is so relaxing
Another challenge to solve
That'll make me grow

Another larger question
That will make me whole

Being fearless is so relaxing

The truth is always there
It's up to you to find it

Don't be afraid,
You'll be amazed at what is true

The Difference it will make
And that's why

Being fearless is so relaxing
Intellectually, it's never been so
Fascinating

The meat-eating sharks
That were circling you

Turn out to be
The parts in your life
You refused to see

Once you see them for
What they truly are

They vanish from your fantasy
And become something you can use
Being fearless is so relaxing, for me!

– Wade Hubbard

Pruning

Conscious evolutionary pruning is similar to inner weeding. Another impact of a golden thread calling and unique capability going unnoticed is a tendency to compensate for the pain by adopting a self-serving ambition. Obsessiveness and unquenchable thirst for control and success, however, become like an unpruned plant—consuming an entire garden and suffocating that which is love-guided. Pruning, therefore, could be described as an act of tough love, with the conscious evolutionary process of metamorphosis increasing the expression of what is vital, universal, and whole-oriented. Ambition, on the other hand, focuses on maintaining the overpowering or unpruned nature of the caterpillar separated self. Inner pruning not only liberates the butterfly. A conscious evolutionary desire to see, be, and become a consequence of a cultivated subconscious, will snip whatever is in excess of a coevolutionary impulse and attraction and let its mask fall. What remains is the butterfly-face and the elegant lines of a universal self-guided life.

Harvest time

The harvest of inner gardening is abundant with transformations on personal, social, environmental, and planetary levels. It is what is gleaned from having formed a set of new coevolutionary relationships, which includes the impersonal and compassionate re-experiencing of yourself. The fruits are the result of acting on a universal and compelling personal instinctual and emotional reaction to ecological energetic feedback. The harvest is the reward of choosing to identify with and join Nature's world of mutual sustainability. Inner gardening plants her earth-seed, because we come from Nature, and it germinates, takes root, and bears its fruit in the communal garden of middle earth—in the fertile zone of body and heart awareness. Middle earth is a symbol for the multi-sensory environment where we can connect and coordinate with a mutually supportive planetary system. It is also therefore a sanctuary, like a protective cocoon, where a synthesis of personal and universal causes become intertwined. You can think of it as where we develop into expressions of the union, and the husk of the separated self disappears as it dissolves in the environment of love. The harvest is a reflection of what happens in the garden of the subconscious, which is also middle earth and the love-filled cocoon of personal integration. The abundance of the harvest includes coming out of the cocoon of the subconscious, a butterfly. Its emergence is also the fruiting of a world-tree-of-life, another name for what replaces a separate identity. The atmosphere at harvest time, in its own rite is transformational. It is the evocative ambience of combined experiences of goodness, truth, and beauty. Harvest time is when the invisible work with a passionate, compassionate, intimate, and humble cycle of conscious evolutionary gardening becomes apparent.

Ritual Composting

The subconscious is sacred ground between Nature and all possible transformations from the human soil of cultivated multi-perceptual awareness. Christopher Bamford identifies the *primacy of the in-between*. It is the psychological open space you created with tilling. At the end of a garden cycle, the season's guiding insight gets *ritually composted*. The "spent" meme is immediately turned back into the soil. This chore is a choice to let go of what had worked in the past. It makes sure the middle earth of the subconscious will remain vital and alive to our senses. New impulses and attractions can surface unobstructed of weeds and separated thinking. Continuing to respond to each new cue supports the thermodynamic phases of a personal conscious evolution through the entire uphill / downhill momentum of a cycle. Bamford, as did Paul Crutzen, Jacob Needleman, and Ervin Laszlo, warns us: we could lose the world if we obstruct the whole message that tingles with hope in between what is understood rationally and a coevolutionary multi-perceptual awareness.

> Alchemy and Hermeticism (an ancient understanding of *the ensouled universe*) are about the primacy of the in-between. Reality and healing and transformation and creation and art are the in-between, the both-and. And to the extent that we lose the ability to be in-between, we lose the world, and, for now, we have lost the ability to be in-between, and we have lost the world.[30]

~ Your LifeBook Journal

A cycle of inner gardening is an all-in-one transformational process. It is very difficult to see we are influencing the direction of evolution when responding affects the equally invisible ecological principles of coevolution. Inner gardening not only matters to us individually, as it did for Wade. It supports a simultaneous unfolding of personal and planetary metamorphosis. The thermodynamic phases of a cycle of inner gardening wax and wane with our subconscious mood swings. As you cultivate unfamiliar, and even existentially challenging, revelations – as you also transform into someone new – does this inspire awe, with realizing how an entire world comes into being via the impersonal coevolutionary aspect of a personal desire to never let go of your thread? Miracles could be the crop of your backyard earthy subconscious. Is it possible to imagine choosing a life of conscious evolutionary gardening, which takes place wherever you go and germinates with each choice you water with a leap of faith?

---

30 Christopher Bamford, "Green Hermeticism" (David Levi Strauss with Peter Lamborn Wilson and Christopher Bamford), *The Brooklyn River Rail* online, January 18, 2018, 15.

Chapter X
Conscious Evolutionary Gardening: Tapestry of Thought

What are the ecological patterns giving rise to the flowers and fruits of the harvest of a cycle of conscious evolutionary gardening? John Dewey, who wrote *Art As Experience*, as paraphrased by poet Mel Elberg, compares understanding how to grow flowers with appreciating art. Both require a passionate apprehending. Inner gardening is guided by seven desire-prompted thermodynamic responses to the artistic universal sensibility and the knots, weeds, trauma, and ambitions of the self-serving, wounded self. If you wish to understand how to cultivate transformations, it is a choice to never lose touch with middle earth—the primacy of the in-between. A decision to get into its emotional humus is not only how to make contact with our multi-perceptual butterfly. Responding multi-perceptually is how to nurture it into being, as well as everything that its emergence will pave on its coevolutionary pathway.

> Anyone can appreciate the beauty of blooming daisies. But if you want to grow daisies, you have to know about the complex relationships between soil, water, and time, and sunlight, in other words, you have to: "apprehend them no longer curiously, but passionately."[31]

---

31 Mel Elberg, *The Brooklyn Rail*, April 2018, 70. Paraphrases John Dewey, *Art As Experience* (New York, NY: Penguin Books, 1934).

Gardening the subconscious is a great analogy for transformational potentials that need to be cultivated and tended just like seeds and plants of a physical garden. The chores, which take place over the course of a conscious evolutionary growing season, are emotionally guided. The momentum is fueled by a passionate apprehension of mysterious impulses and attractions. Trusting and choosing to have faith in the direction they provide will require additional gusts of emotions for staying in the uphill / downhill thermodynamic pulse of a personal conscious evolution. Without the experiences of intimacy, compassion, and humility, we lack the type of energy needed for making a decision to change unsustainable but familiar patterns of life. The adjustments, however, reflect compatibility with fundamental principles. A passionate apprehension and compassionate response to these suddenly becomes a multi-perceptual reflex to our relationship with Nature. Out of the complex soil of personal turmoil and flashes of intuition, there is a yet to be discovered, lived, and unwritten book of a whole-oriented human purpose—its wanting seed awaits a multi-perceptual response to be able to germinate in the emotional ground of the subconscious.

When there are no human coevolutionary perspectives, it becomes necessary to weave its tapestry of thought. The focus of Part Three is to use the groundwork of the evolutionary and conscious evolutionary perspectives, which were developed earlier, to leverage a coevolutionary personal understanding. Let us weave its tapestry of thought, making connections between the focuses of the chores and their compatibility with specific ecological principles. This is complex—a multi-perceptual universal self-impulse and attraction has *both* a personal *and* impersonal purpose.

I discovered the book *The Way Life Works* by Mahlon Hoagland and Bert Dodson while homeschooling Renée. It begins with sixteen ecological patterns; the conscious evolutionary gardening chores are a human interpretation. I was struck by how their message expressed the wisdom of the unwritten book of life. This is also to say, they reflect what it means to live universal self-conscious. The principles are what one observes when the purpose is whole-oriented. Thus, they reflect the unique conscience of a passionate apprehension that could not only grow daisies, but also a world that could work well for most who are living in it. It is the butterfly and reality, that the agency of relating – in between the hardpan crust and the silent fragrance of multi-perceptual consciousness – could cultivate and plant. Our tapestry will weave in **ecological thought-strands,** portraying the vital connections and relationships between inner gardening and living ecologically. Midway through, the ecological thought-strands will be exchanged for **mystical thought-strands,** which affirm *the harvest* reaped from a cycle of inner gardening. The **coevolutionary strands** will weave connections between personal experiences and the ecological and mystical interpretations of the energetic patterns we silently sense are percolating with the whole message in the soil of the subconscious.

Ecological Thought-Strand:

Life Works in Cycles: A Circular Flow of Information

> Life loves loops...Loops tame uncontrolled events. One-way processes, given sufficient energy and materials, tend to "run away," to go faster and faster unless they are inhibited or restrained...The system self-corrects; the parts self-adjust. If such self-generated restraints and inducements occur in small steps, the overall system appears to maintain itself in a steady state. Every biological circuit, whether a sequence of proteins in the act of consuming a sugar molecule or a complex ecosystem exchanging material and energy, exhibits self-correcting tendencies...Information flows around the circuit and feeds back to the starting point, making necessary adjustments along the way. It's easier to understand how molecular systems assemble into complicated, apparently purposeful organisms when we look at events in terms of multi-layered loops of control

and creation—and substitute the term "self-correcting" for "purposeful."[32]

Coevolutionary Strand:

The seven garden chores follow the adjusting phases of Nature's loop-pattern. Planting and watering are in step with the energetic thermodynamic expanding phase of a loop cycle. Tilling, weeding, pruning, and composting, on the other hand, shift gears with a universal self-correcting response. The garden chores compose a cycle of self-generated restraints and inducements and, being seven different focuses, the responses occur in small steps. A life of inner gardening is a continuous universal self-correcting process. It may be how to experience a resonant (steady) state of a coevolutionary life. Following the pattern, therefore, is purposeful whether you wish to grow flowers or a sustainable future. Both require staying passionately in the loop of Nature's self-correcting pattern.

Ecological Thought-Strand:

Life is Opportunistic: Making the Most of What Is

> Life's universal tendency to "make do" with whatever is available in its surroundings... Opportunists don't wait around for the right conditions. They adapt to what is, and they make use of whatever they find around them.[33]

Coevolutionary Strand:

The garden of the subconscious, which travels with us, provides endless opportunities to collaborate with Nature. If What Is, we are too, then making the most of who we are could be to water with a

---

32 Mahlon Hoagland and Bert Dodson, *The Way Life Works* (New York, NY: Three Rivers Press, 1995), 21.
33 Ibid., 28.

leap of faith in its transcendent understanding. A golden thread establishes a personal relationship with what is—and responding is how we transform into coevolutionary pathways. We do not have to look beyond our subconscious to discover how we could make a remarkable difference in the world. Nature, too, may view this opportunistically.

Ecological Thought-Strand:

Life is Interconnected and Interdependent:
A Network of Interactions

> Look at the coral reef as a multilevel, integrated system. Ultimately, everything in the reef connects with everything else. The survival of the reef shark is closely tied to the survival of the coral polyp, even though the two may have no contact and certainly no awareness of each other. What survives and evolves are patterns of organization—the organism plus its strategies for making a living and for fitting in. Any successful change of strategy by one organism will create a ripple or adjustments in the reef community. Called coevolution, this is the kind of creative force at work everywhere life has taken hold.[34]

Coevolutionary Strand:

A passionate and compassionate inner gardening technique could be critical to resolving homelessness, reversing the deterioration of human and natural environments. Weeding a separated identity takes a stand for what is whole and its ripple effect could ensure, as previously mentioned—*a reef shark, a child, a person who is homeless, a mother, an artist, a sea turtle, a salamander, along with the rest of the living world, will benefit rather than become harmed by our activities.* Cultivating

---

34 Ibid., 33.

multi-perceptual awareness makes it impossible to turn a blind eye to the fate of other strands in the web of life. Visceral and emotional activation suddenly reveals the following truth: other strands weave our essential being and their vibrations sustain us energetically. The subconscious is in our own backyard and when it is attended to by responding multi-perceptually, it becomes an organic way to live interdependently. A mirrored personal reflection of the process, however, is we transform into coevolutionary *actants: who never really act alone. Its efficacy or agency always depends on the collaboration, cooperation, or interactive interference of many bodies and forces.*[35] We lay our subconscious earth bare when non-subjective impulses and attractions allow its fertile scent of silence to fill our imaginations with more meaning to being human and alive.

Ecological Thought-Strand:

Life Tends to Optimize Rather than Maximize

> To optimize means to achieve just the right amount—a value in the middle range between too much and too little...At the level of the organism, optimizing is an intricate dance involving many interacting parts and values...maximizing any single value (i.e., pushing it to the extreme) tends to reduce flexibility in the overall system, so that it may not be able to adapt to adverse environmental change...Maximizing can be seen as a form of addiction...Humans exhibit addictive tendencies when trying to maximize such values as wealth, pleasure, security, and power. In restoring optimal balance, we might well take note of nature's dictum: Too much of a good thing is not a good thing.[36]

---

35 Jane Bennett, *Vibrant Matter: A Political Ecology of Things* (Durham, NC: Duke University Press, 2010), 21.
36 Hoagland and Dodson, 26.

Coevolutionary Strand:

Inner pruning could be a direct response to this pattern. It snips anything in excess of a thin golden thread fiber. It is the invisible line between our personal world and the bigger picture of coevolutionary interdependence. Never letting go of the thread is how to find the sweet spot, staying limber and flexible to respond either passionately or compassionately on an as-need-be basis. In either case, the reactions are appropriate and foster a deeper coevolutionary conscience. This grounded stance automatically ensures social, global, environmental, and planetary responsibility. The sweet spot is *located* in the sacred earth of the primacy of the in-between. Here is where the whole message filters through the layers of congested stress with a passionate apprehension. The thermodynamics of remaining flexible and responsive is how we cultivate the new tendency to optimize. It is also the back and forth flow of the universal self-correcting loop. Never letting go of the thread is a passionate leap of faith. However, we bounce back to compassionately heal personal fears, obsessions, addictions, and compulsions. This is the coevolutionary perspective for reclaiming our lives, and by extension, rejuvenating everything else that is a consequence of personal suffering.

Ecological Thought-Strand:

Life Maintains itself by Turnover: Put It Together—Take It Apart

> To exist, life requires organization. Organization requires energy…In turnover we can sense life's need for a continuous "flow through" of energy. A high-information / high-energy state must be dynamically maintained by the ceaseless building and destroying, ordering and disordering, of life's parts.[37]

---

37 Ibid., 25.

Coevolutionary Strand:

Conscious evolutionary tilling, weeding, pruning, and ritual composting perform the existential challenge through enacting the pattern turnover. Understanding it is for the sake of maintaining a high energy flow in both the gardener's life and the world around us: this coevolutionary perspective casts a meaningful and hopeful interpretation. The pattern turnover is invisible until we develop a (ceaseless) supple flexibility with an evolved responsive attitude. Its transformational effects become visible as we carry it out via a conscious evolutionary decluttering and revitalizing of a whole integrated universal self-experience. When we act on the entire sensation, we are also nurturing Earth's garden. On the other hand, the task of turning under fragments of a once impenetrable identity also liberates the butterfly self who was blocked by its opacity.

Change the Strands

Let us exchange the ecological thought-strands for mystical threads that describe a human experience of the effects of responding to the patterns. A visceral and emotional sensation of these, however, reliably becomes interpreted as revealing a universal self. Its unveiling includes patterns that, when followed, are also reliably considered transformational.

Mystical Thought-Strand:

Fourteenth-century monk and mystic Meister Eckhart believes Nature "secretly chooses" to *ferret out the track in which God may be found*—rather than relying on more materialistic approaches to procuring food, drink, clothing, and a life of comfort. Eckhart may be celebrating the "harvest" from following his subconscious' inner guidance. He also affirms the level of meaning in the experience, when it becomes interpreted as revealing God.

Meister Eckhart:

Nature's intent is neither food, nor drink nor clothing, nor comfort, nor anything else from which God is left out. Whether you like it or not, whether you know it or not, secretly Nature seeks and hunts and tries to ferret out the track in which God may be found.[38]

Mystical Thought-Strand:

Second-century gnostic teacher Valentinus illuminates Nature's opportunistic pattern that makes the *most of what is*. He may have come to the same conclusion as John Dewey, but centuries earlier. Whether you are growing flowers or cultivating universal self-awareness, both require the comprehensive attention of a passionate apprehension. Valentinus not only apprehends the presence of our eternal being, but also the crisis of being *thrown* into a world where it is unknown. An entire cycle of inner gardening rotates with the momentum of the push and pull—dynamics of becoming multi-perceptually universal self-conscious *and* integrated with and by the understanding.

Valentinus:

What makes us free is the knowledge who we were, what we have become; where we were, wherein we have been thrown; whereto we speed, wherefrom we are redeemed; what is birth and what rebirth.[39]

---

38 Meister Eckhart, cited in *The Perennial Philosophy* by Aldous Huxley (New York, NY: Harper Perennial Modern Classics, 1945), 66.
39 Hans Jonas, essay "Gnosticism and Modern Nihilism" in *The Allure of Gnosticism: The Gnostic Experience in Jungian Psychology and Contemporary Culture* by Robert Segal (Peru, IL: Open Court Publishing, 1995), 130.

Mystical Thought-Strand:

Luke, writer of one of the Gospels, affirms the transformational harvest from diligent inner gardening. Jacqueline Baldet also reaped the benefits by never letting go of her thread. Discovering your life is taking care of itself is a sign of having slipped into the world of mutual sustainability. It is an existence fully in step with these patterns and a labor of love that expresses beauty.

Luke:

> Consider the lilies how they grow: they toil not, they spin not; and yet I say unto you, that Solomon in all his glory was not arrayed like one of these.[40]

Mystical Thought-Strand:

Jean-Yves Leloup asks the question: *How can we live fully the consequences* of our universal and personal self. Inner gardening is a possible answer. A choice to surrender to the expansive and healing phases of a cycle is how we become conduits for transformations, and a consequence of cultivating multi-perceptual universal self-awareness.

Jean-Yves Leloup:

> Within us we contain both the uncreated and the eternal, the divine and the human. Where does one begin and the other end? ... How can we live fully the consequences of the theanthropic wedding of created and uncreated?[41]

---

40 Luke: 12: 27, *The Holy Bible*, King James Version (London, New York, Toronto: Oxford University Press, 1611), 1323.

41 Leloup, *The Gospel of Thomas*, 111.

~ Your LifeBook Journal

Imagine you have entered a large revolving door like those at museums and department stores. As it turns around in a loop, experience the phases of a cycle of inner gardening. Similar to how a caterpillar transforms, everything for which living the patterns has provided its coevolutionary pathway will appear silently like a butterfly on the other side of the doorway. It is a consequence of the invisible, but highly responsive, conscious evolutionary work—destroying, reordering, ordering, and rebuilding a universal self-guided life from the ground of the subconscious, up into daily life. The coronavirus has served this destructive purpose, being an active force of evolution. A passionate apprehension and compassionate response to energetic feedback on our coevolutionary relationship could, however, become a catalyst for a higher level of order and harmony through the *composted* parts from yesterday's world. Where do you sense and feel your personal and coevolutionary work begin and the other end? Could you embrace them as being one and the same purpose?

Chapter XI
Four Woven Swatches

Swatch #1

My childhood golden thread attraction to Nature took form when I discovered my capability for weaving. The craft is a fractal of ecological principles such as the (purposeful) self-correcting loop pattern. Plying the horizontal moving weft strand with the vertical warp threads, which are set up onto the loom, is a repeated pattern that ensures a fabric or tapestry becomes whole. Its tactility, sensuousness, and oscillating rhythm also communicate the thermodynamic seasons of ordering and reordering.

Swatch #2

Weaving became more than a craft when I felt it was animating and coordinating me in the loop of coevolution. This experience transformed the idea of a career in weaving to becoming a labor of love. Thus, my personal work and engaging in an interdependent process were considered one and the same. A shift in focus – from producing a good to listening with a multi-sensory experience to the touch and feel of the process – allowed for a passionate apprehension of the bigger universal picture of weaving. Its integrative technology transformed it into a process-based non-verbal medium, communicating the wisdom of the unwritten book. Its tactile connectivity demonstrated universal self-awareness. It also materializes the perspective becoming a real fabric or tapestry. Weaving and relating multi-perceptually share common elements: they both express, at the same time, what they see, say, and physically manifest. The craft, just as is true when responding to Nature's impulse and attraction, are integrative processes that communicate the same whole message.

Swatch #3

From an early age I knew that I was an artist. Besides choosing weaving as a medium that resembled Nature's world, built into its integrative process is a *whole-oriented conscience*. A concept for a tapestry image, I believe, expresses a truth if it can be translated into woven form. My artistic themes have been influenced by my parents' ideas. What is the meaning of our powers that can serve a greater good, or what is an image that would fit human capabilities—these have been part of my golden thread calling to explore. As memes, however, there is an arbitrariness with no underlying conscience to guide a whole-oriented purpose. My woven medium, embodying process and concern for the whole fabric, is also its message. I use the integrity of its built-in conscience to adjust my textile images to reflect the feedback.

Swatch #4

I discovered one day I was "offering up" personal issues to the rhythmic cyclic flow of the weaving process. These related to my wounded separated self who tended to feel a victim of circumstance, such as a lack of appreciation in the world for my labors of love. I would "float" the discordant vibration over the harmonious patterns of weaving. It immediately exposed a personal misconception—something that I had refused to see, as Wade expressed in his poem. Without leaving my loom, I would experience the no-conflict law, as I adjusted a personal sense of separation with the universal and ecologically similar weaving process.

The four Swatches are short stories about another human activity, like gardening, which shares similarities with ecological processes. Weaving and gardening, therefore, provide apt analogies in understanding the binary effects of a personal integration process that simultaneously serves a coevolutionary function. Let's take stock of the four Swatch themes: A thermodynamic rhythm, a labor of love, the medium is also the message, the patterning process enforces a conscience with considering the good of the larger whole, plus the no-conflict law and the track where God could be found, as Meister Eckhart described. The swatches belong to a much bigger fabric than merely a personal musing. They are of a piece when you are relating multi-perceptually. Its instinctual and emotional responsiveness to invisible energetic patterns, passionately apprehended and embodied, organically conforms to how Nature: tends to evolve thermodynamically, cares for her world as a labor of love when nobody is paying her to sustain our lives, expresses the whole message at all times, and non-locally transforms as if by magic.

~ Your LifeBook Journal

The Swatches echo the story-mirrors in Part One. Their subject could persist as inconsequential Sunday paper personal interest features. However, when you have evolutionary and coevolutionary perspectives to evaluate scenarios, such as the short stories about physical and metaphysical weaving in the Swatches, you have the basis of a highly consequential transformational strategy. The *consequential* handlooming and multi-perceptual inner weaving patterns are invisible, as too are the patterns in Nature that are affected. Therefore, the extent of the impact that choosing to respond to multi-perceptual awareness could have on our surroundings is unknown and the results express Nature being us doing her work. The point of this book is to make connections with initially unconscious tendencies to respond and also to identify the effects, so that our cooperative relationship becomes apparent. Inner gardening took a multi-perceptual coevolutionary perspective on a *simulated* test drive. It was a fast-forward look—what if you kept responding, after a passionate apprehending of your golden threaded coevolutionary connection with other creature-weavers and doers, the invisible work of mutual sustainability. It could result in a personal metamorphosis into the butterfly of an evolutionary pathway. It could share the impersonal identity with a new earth, emerging from the unblocked or opened space, as you cultivated their transformational seeds with a conscious evolutionary, inner alignment. Are you experiencing, as its needle falls through a small crack in the sky, your potency to affect the unseen energetic and quantum ground—before it hits bottom, on top of the wire-grass, and becomes lost in its *haystack* of other concerns?

Chapter XII
Conscious Evolutionary Weaving

The subconscious is unconscious because rarely do our three brains integrate with multi-perceptual awareness. The three-brain system – the basic, limbic, and neocortex – is a coevolutionary inner loom. It weaves with the same responsive process that guides the complex sequence of garden chores. The source of the guidance is the invisible patterns of coevolution, which underlie human instinctual and emotional universal self-impulses and attractions. A passionate apprehending of these is the catalyzer to awakening and activating the multi-perceptual subconscious. Its impersonal function is when it reveals our unique relationship with the cosmos of interdependent relationships—while at the same time it gets us involved. The revelatory lens is a woven synthesis of the basic, limbic, and neocortex brain systems. For reasons unknown, the neocortex interprets a passionate (limbic) apprehension of (basic brain) feedback from the invisible patterns, the transcendent universal self. Therefore, its desire-prompted / process-based counterpart provides the link between us and our potential to become universal self-conscious and guided. If knowing and living this is how we coevolve, then we will also experience the invisible phenomena that Nature uses to manifest or incorporate a species' coevolutionary strategy into new physical realities. In this perspective, there is a connection between becoming multi-perceptually responsive, and that state ultimately leading to living interdependently. Replacing an exploitative with a symbiotic relationship, therefore, could lessen living from paycheck to paycheck.

Passion becomes compassion, intimacy, and humility with the conscious evolutionary healing and expanding to intellectualized universal self-feedback. This describes the process of relating multi-perceptually. And, when it reliably unveils our truth, while we are responding and becoming a personal expression, it is also coevolutionary. We have only done a swift test-drive of this idea's knotted thought-strands and handspun perspectives. Our mystery, and *the mystery*, to be explored further in this chapter is: what happens when we become actants in the thermodynamic mass murmuration of coevolutionary life weavers and dancers? The *tiny pin-head* on the needle falling from the crack in the sky, gleaming with the potency to affect the unseen energetic and quantum ground, is how pure expressions of love – such as a passionate apprehension, compassion, intimacy, humility, goodness, truth, and beauty – constitute the *affecting or effective* transformational / coevolutionary ingredient.

What are the phenomena that, becoming reconciled with the patterns, activate their transformational effects? Weaving the inner loom involves the same conscious evolutionary responses as gardening the multi-perceptual subconscious. Therefore, this chapter explores the invisible patterns that inspire universal-self awareness, and – when its feedback becomes life-guiding – are responsible for "the miracles."

We will weave a richly brocaded tapestry of thought, in lieu of there being no coevolutionary human perspective. It will connect the dots and knots between a love-guided multi-perceptual awareness and its transformational impacts on the quantum ground. The tapestry shows we truly are *both* the medium *and* the message—we are mutually related. Its embodied gnosis amps up with a creational love-vibration. The tiny fluctuation, created by thinking with the heart, *collapses* a like reality, which celebrates the whole message— we are mutually defining. A golden thread expression proliferates invisibly when it *propagates in all directions at the same time.* Collapse is a quantum mechanical term for the transition from a non-physical quantum state to a physical manifestation.

The Four Woven Swatches provided a "diamond in the rough" portrait of handweaving's non-local effects due to its close ties with ecological principles. Weaving our three brains into one mind, body, heart awareness is a metaphysical version, whose transformational potentials are related to the same unpolished diamond. Our tapestry of thought will polish the mossy wire-grass thinking off of its multi-perceptual surface. Weaving connections will expose the hidden gem of our three brains. Learning how to weave its loom will get us in touch with our quantum anatomy, such as our pure state and wave-face. However, the inner weaving process itself can non-locally affect the direction of evolution. Perhaps the more accurate explanation: it could collapse an alternative to a mass extinction, the seed to which coexists with the current world destined to fail.

The first half of our tapestry of thought will make connections between what our three brains can neurologically relate to, and when they do, I will identify the cosmic, non-local phenomena directly impacted. To show this relationship, our tapestry will include neurological, ecological, biophysical, and quantum mechanical **Scientific Thought-Strands.** The second part of the tapestry switches an objective view, in the next chapter, for mystical experiences of what has been described. The **Mystical Thought-Strands** reveal the potentials for becoming integrated, which include discovering you are *receiving help from the elements of Nature.* They affirm that trusting and having faith in a love-guided response, to what was quantum mechanically expressed, could invisibly or non-locally transform. Both types of thought-strands will be woven with a **Coevolutionary Perspective**, when neither the scientific nor mystical outlooks imagine this human potential. Use your intuition to weave the warp and weft strands of the tapestry. It is your experience of what is being described that is most useful in discovering the huge diamond in the rough of a collective unrealized potential to effect radical change.

Tapestry of Thought

Scientific Thought-Strand

Coevolutionary Perspective: Neurologist Elaine de Beauport acknowledges our whole brain-mind-body complex vibrates and therefore could redefine us as energetic beings. This is also life's common ground and thus creates a bond with everything that reflects the shared universal self. A resonant response is how to orchestrate a multi-perceptual understanding. Were this also to be responded to, the meaning of being human would be redefined—at the same time as becoming its expression, it would have an impact on the future. We could become identified with what our instincts and heart know energetically more than with what is possible rationally, and is often unresponsive.

Elaine de Beauport: Neurological Thought-Strand

> Energy is now our common ground. As human matter we vibrate, the control panels we call our brain systems vibrate, and our whole brain-mind-body vibrates. We are energy beings. This is even more descriptive of us and our potential future than saying we are human beings. It is energy and vibration that now unite us, whether through visible or invisible wavelengths. Our three brain systems have always orchestrated the human being.[42]

Scientific Thought-Strand

Coevolutionary Perspective: De Beauport affirms the significance of a passionate apprehension that engages the inner loom of multi-perceptual awareness. The limbic system allows us to become emotionally affected by pure energetic feedback from the

---

42 Elaine de Beauport, *The Three Faces of Mind: Developing your Mental, Emotional, and Behavioral Intelligences* (Wheaton, IL: Theosophical Publishing House, 1996), 326.

basic brain, which receives the digital message—we "incorporate the universe." She does not seem confident we will express this identity any time soon, however. This may be on account of lacking a coevolutionary perspective. Or, maybe it is not understood that Nature is experimenting with a species who can become universal self-conscious. The big question that we are asking is: what if we choose to fully respond? Perhaps this is what Nature is also waiting to find out.

Neurological Thought-Strand: Elaine de Beauport

> *With our limbic system:* we can feel some aspects of the universe. This means we allow ourselves to be affected by something and to receive feedback emotionally... *With our basic brain:* we incorporate the universe. We receive feedback at a vibrational level, sensorial and cellular. This means that vibrations literally affect our basic and physical structures. There is a stimulus from our environment and a response from our nervous system, whether or not we can feel that response in our limbic system or are able to reflect on that response in our neocortex.[43]

Scientific Thought-Strand

Coevolutionary Perspective: Mae-Wan Ho explains the thermodynamic pulse that circulates energy and information through the web of cells of the biosphere. Our Nature-given, basic brain is constantly monitoring and reacting to the force of the pulse. She (Nature) *hopes* a passionate apprehension will guide us into the larger oscillating flow of ordering and reordering our lives ecologically. Ho names the invisible oscillation pattern and the pair of thermodynamic dance partners, the *organizer* and the *organized*. One partner is the non-physical energetic patterns (the universal

---

43 Ibid., 327.

self-experience) and the other a living organism, such as humans. The pulse of the thermodynamic rhythm is slightly out-of-kilter—and we can also experience this. For example, when Renée and I were gardening, I experienced tilling my blocked experiences of separation as an uphill effort, while a choice to heal with a leap of faith had a quicker tempo.

Ecological and Biophysical Thought-Strands: Mae-Wan Ho

> The concept of energy flow in biology is familiar to every biochemist and ecologist...Accompanying the energy flow is *cycling* of materials through the biosphere: carbon dioxide, water, nitrogen, sulphates and phosphates are 'fixed' by green plants and bacteria into high electronic energy compounds which cycle through the bodies of animals in the biosphere before they are broken down and returned to the soil and the atmosphere for general recycling... (Cycling and re-cycling are indeed nature's way).[44]...This intimate relationship between energy flow and the cycling of the elements turns out not to be at all fortuitous. For it is the energy flow which organizes the material system, taking it far away from thermodynamic equilibrium by raising its energy level, producing gradients, and cyclic flow patterns of materials (and energy), in short, generating a hierarchy of space-time structures which in turn organizes the energy flow. The key to life is in this mutuality of spontaneous relationship between the system and the environment, each in turn the organizer and the organized.[45]

---

44 Mae-Wan Ho, *The Rainbow and the Worm: The Physics of Organisms*, 2nd Edition (Singapore World Scientific Publishing, 1998), 38.
45 Ibid., 39.

Scientific Thought-Strand

Coevolutionary Perspective: De Beauport reveals our brain's potential to respond to quantum realities, whose phenomena most closely express universal self-awareness. She reiterates environmental philosopher Baird Callicott's description of a mutually supportive web of different species' strands. De Beauport explains we are being sustained by the vibrations of other life forms. She implies we have the brain power necessary to consciously participate in coevolving the earth and cosmos. Not only could inner weaving suffice in orchestrating our whole physical and energetic quality of being—the integrative and conscious evolutionary orchestrating process doubles as the *how to* coevolve.

Neurological Thought-Strand: Elaine de Beauport

> What was formerly called the unconscious now is called the limbic brain and the basic brain, filtering various wavelengths of energy, including quantum realities...If we wish to acknowledge or indeed if we have experienced clues that there is much more of this cosmos than we are fully feeling or able to express, we must also realize that while we are alive, we are living in this cosmos, not only expressing but also receiving and being sustained by all other life-vibrations...As live energy systems, we are being sustained by vibrations that have made the earth and the cosmos and that are still engaged in the process. It is for us to join the process consciously.[46]

Scientific Thought-Strand

Coevolutionary Perspective: Mae-Wan Ho adds a touch of intimacy to the dance between organizer and organized with *symmetrical coupling*. She emphasizes the radical "fairness" of the

---

46 de Beauport, 326-327.

relationship. The responses to each other are mutually beneficial. This is why a leap of faith and getting swept up in the coevolutionary dance will never leave you falling flat on your face. Instead, a choice to organize your next dance move, like jumping to Vashon, or choosing to come from the bigger picture, could be reciprocated with the gift of a future that is liberating or more relaxing. Weaving the inner loom is how to join a symmetrically equitable coevolutionary economy that expands with giving and receiving. The "receiving" could, for example, be the experience of the no-conflict law. Symmetrical coupling expresses Nature's love compatibility and thus a full conscious evolutionary response creates a human link with expressions of passion, compassion, intimacy, and humility. The resonant quality of love penetrates physical, energetic, and quantum layers within our own human fabric and the larger whole where its swatchlette is cozily embedded. We can experience symmetrical coupling with the patterns of the transcendent universal self through a conscious evolutionary response to its desire-prompted counterpart. It is the romantic thermodynamics of the coevolutionary dance, when we organize *with* Nature and then the rhythm changes direction as we become organized *by* her response to us.

Biophysical Thought-Strand: Mae-Wan Ho

> Symmetrical coupling involves a complete reciprocity, so that the effects of one process on the other are the same, and furthermore, they can reverse roles so the giver of the energy becomes the receiver and vice versa.[47]

---

[47] Mae-Wan Ho, *Coherent Energy, Liquid Crystallinity and Acupuncture*, talk presented to the British Acupuncture Society, 2 October 1999 (The Institute of Science in Society, http://www.i-sis.org.uk/freewill.shtml), accessed 5/27/2009.

Scientific Thought-Strand

Coevolutionary Perspective: Mae-Wan Ho explains, if you wish to understand organisms, including us, it is necessary to become acquainted with electromagnetic theory of light and matter and the laws of thermodynamics. These are examples of invisible phenomena which, when passionately apprehended, are multi-perceptually interpreted as universal self-awareness. However, a full response organically gets us into the uphill / downhill rhythm of the thermodynamic personal conscious evolution. It is also the same ebb and flow of handweaving and its metaphysical conscious evolutionary version. The information of the 16 patterns electro-magnetically and thermodynamically circulate the entire web of cells in the biosphere. A cycle of inner gardening and weaving is the experience of the slightly out of equilibrium thermodynamics of expanding and adjusting to the patterns. There is another important piece to understanding a universal process. A multi-perceptual universal self-response adds a human layer to our reacting to a life-wide phenomenon. The rhythm of a coevolutionary response multi-tasks. It compels the romantic back and forth relationship between organized and organizer. We engage in the relationship by following a golden thread calling because its impulse is how we "organize" something new in the world. And, when we respond multi-perceptually, it is *both* a process of understanding, *and* its uphill / downhill universal self-correcting process is how we join the big dance of coevolution with the larger whole. Multiple transformational effects reveal some of inner weaving's diamond in the rough. Certainly, these dynamic vibrations were the ones that I was offering up – my experiences of separation, while I was weaving on my loom – with the hope of these becoming healed. There is another piece to the puzzle as to how the healings miraculously take place. It could be attributed to the love frequencies attending a multi-perceptual response. These could resonate as well as activate the non-local wave embedded in the electromagnetic flow.

Biophysical Thought-Strand

Mae-Wan Ho:

The two great unifying concepts in physics and chemistry that are most relevant for understanding the organism are the laws of thermodynamics and the electromagnetic theory of light and matter... electromagnetic energy animates and coordinates the living system. Electromagnetic theory also places both light and matter within the central conundrum of the wave particle duality of physical reality.[48]

Scientific Thought-Strand

Coevolutionary Perspective: Ervin Laszlo identifies the intangible wave aspect of the tangible universe, which our instincts and emotions react to. The phenomenon exists in the electromagnetic flow and its divine-like quality could be what we instinctually and emotionally desire to become its animated and coordinated expression. His quantum mechanical explanation is as unworldly as a passionate universal self-apprehension. We are, as are all organisms, *integrated macroscopic quantum systems*. The wave mirrors the invisible phenomenon non-local coherence. It influences the ecological ripple effect of coevolution. The potential for becoming universal self-conscious and guided could be that the effects *propagate in all directions at the same time.*

Quantum Mechanical Thought-Strand

Ervin Laszlo:

The living organism is not a mechanistic system where genetic instructions are rigorously transcribed into

---

48 Ho, *The Rainbow and the Worm*, 95-96.

molecular structure. Rather, the organism is a highly integrated system where self-maintaining processes engage all levels simultaneously, from the microscopic to the molecular and macroscopic. Adjustments, responses, and changes required for the maintenance of the system propagate in all directions at the same time and are sensitively tuned to conditions in the organism's environment.[49] The living organism is in some respects a "macroscopic quantum system."[50] The German theoretician Marco Bischof summed up the insight emerging at the frontiers of the life sciences. "Quantum mechanics has established the primacy of the inseparable whole. For this reason...the basis of the new biophysics must be the insight into the fundamental interconnectedness *within* the organism as well as *between* organisms, and that of the organism *with the environment*."[51]

Scientific Thought-Strand
Coevolutionary Perspective: Mae-Wan Ho affirms my daughter Renée's golden thread understanding when each is: a *plurality that is singular, a multiplicity that is a unity*. She goes further in describing organisms, which include us—neurologically sensitive to the part of us that is *a domain of coherence, a pure state of pure duration that permeates the whole of our being*. Gnostic teacher Valentinus believed *knowing who we were and where we came from* is critical to personal well-being. His inner loom must have been resonating with the phenomena Ho describes.

---

49 Laszlo, Ervin, *The Akasha Paradigm: Revolution in Science, Evolution in Consciousness* (Cardiff by the Sea, CA: Waterside Publishing, 2012), 13-14.
50 Laszlo, *Science and the Akashic Field*, 46.
51 Ibid., 49.

Biophysical Thought-Strand: Mae-Wan Ho

Quantum coherence entails a plurality that is singular, a multiplicity that is a unity. The 'self' is the domain of coherence, a pure state of pure duration that permeates the whole of our being.[52]

Scientific Thought-Strand
Coevolutionary Perspective: Ervin Laszlo embellishes Mae-Wan Ho's description with additional revelations. He affirms an entire universe of possibilities is embedded in our middle earth, which Christopher Bamford portrayed as the primacy of the in-between. This sacred space is part of our anatomy, it is the shared quantum ground, and it is *flush* with *virtual states*—these encode all possible realities that could become multi-perceptually apprehended / expressed. Inner gardening and weaving are processes that get us electromagnetically and thermodynamically in between the world created by separated thinking and the future in its embryonic virtual state. Laszlo explains the dynamic relationship between organisms and the highly sensitive virtual states. For example, our love-guided response has agency in the *selecting* of an alternative future that corresponds with a multi-perceptual, embodied universal self-observation. He explains... *every system that emerges in the manifest world represents a selection from among a set of virtual states.* Laszlo goes on to quote physical-chemist Lothar Schäfer's description of the dance and the romance of coevolution as an: *incessant, restless dance* and *at the foundation of things transcendent (that is, virtual) order and real order are interlocked in an uninterrupted frantic embrace.*

---

52 Mae-Wan Ho, *Quantum Coherence and Conscious Experience* (Bioelectrodynamics Laboratory, Open University, Walton Hall, Milton Keys, U.K.) Institute of Science in Society, Kybernetes 26, 265-276, 1997, http://www.i-sis.org.uk/brainde.shtml, 5, accessed 5/27/2009.

Quantum Mechanical Thought-Strand

Ervin Laszlo:

Particles that make up the manifest aspect of reality are not little mass points, like tiny balls of matter, but waves; more exactly, standing waves...All visible order in the universe is determined by the rules that govern the interference of these waves... The kinds of interactions that are possible are determined in turn by the order of virtual states...Every particle, every atom, and every molecule possesses not only the state that it occupies when it is observed, but also states that are empty and hence are said to be "virtual." Virtual states are described by probability functions and bits of information. They become real when a particle, an atom, a molecule "jumps" into them...Every system that emerges in the manifest world represents a selection from among a set of virtual states that is available to it. There is a constant transformation from virtual into real states and also from real into virtual states. Quantum physical-chemist Lothar Schäfer describes this as "an incessant, restless dance" where the occupied states are constantly abandoned and become virtual, while the empty states become occupied and real. As he writes, "At the foundation of things transcendent (that is, virtual) order and real order are interlocked in an uninterrupted frantic embrace."[53]

Scientific Thought-Strand
Coevolutionary Perspective: Seeded in the earth of our subconscious are a dormant crop of virtual states, ready to germinate with embodied self-awareness. The *seeds* encode alternative possibilities to what has been rationally understood. Everything that could become

---

53 Laszlo, *Science and the Akashic Field*, 28-29.

multi-perceptually germinated or selected, *coexists* with the world that is roiling in chaos. Mae-Wan Ho's explanation of the fertile *pure state* reverberates with the experiential, sensual bouquet of silence rising from the tilled earth of the subconscious. A great human mystery of coevolution has remained in an undisturbed – by rational thinking – virtual state. It has been entombed and a fully humanized human has been in a coma for as many years as the inner loom has not been weaving multi-perceptually. The smell, taste, and texture of your *domain of coherence* is palpable. It awaits a full multi-perceptual response to its emotional prompting. Ho echoes archeologist Klaus Schmidt's and Richard Dawkins' sentiments: the power of the mind has agency to "collapse" selected realities. An entire *other* world, another civilization, has yet to be selected. It awaits a passionate apprehension, thus we may frantically embrace its virtual seed in the region of our being that eternally persists—our *indivisible pure state*. Ho affirms we absolutely play a role in the direction that evolution will take.

Biophysical Thought-Strand: Mae-Wan Ho

> The fundamental picture of reality in quantum mechanics is that all alternative possibilities open to the system co-exist in a 'pure state' rather than a mixture of states until the instant when we observe it…A pure state is indivisible, it is a unity which we can represent as a 'superposition' of all the possible alternatives… The act of observation seems to put an end to this dream-like pure state into one of the possibilities that previously existed only as a potential. Hence, the observer seems to somehow determine the fate of the particle by 'collapsing' all its possibilities into a state of definiteness… there is a school of thought that believes that it is the act of observation by the *human* consciousness which makes definite things happen.[54]

---

54 Ho, *The Rainbow and the Worm*, 203.

Science Thought-Strand

Coevolutionary Perspective: Ervin Laszlo refers to a particle physicist whose experiment reveals the transcendent universal self as the *wave-face*. It is more *real* than the familiar "corpuscular" identity. A quantum reflects a complementary corpuscular / wave nature—and so do we.

Quantum Mechanical Thought-Strand: Ervin Laszlo

> Shahriar Afshar, a young Iranian-American physicist, demonstrated that even when the corpuscular face is observed, the wave-aspect is still there...Afshar suggests – and a number of particle physicists are inclined to agree – the wave aspect of the particle is the fundamental aspect. The corpuscular face is not the real face...[55]

~ Your LifeBook Journal

Neurologist Elaine de Beauport has made it clear it is neurologically possible to relate to the phenomena described through the science strands. She expressed skepticism we could become conscious and impelled by the experiences, however. It is a latent coevolutionary potential, which requires a choice to respond. Touch and feel the vibrant textures of your evolutionary, conscious evolutionary, and coevolutionary perspectives. Feel the textural knots or dots between the impulses and attractions that you came into the world with and the non-local phenomena expressing universal self-awareness. Do you see woven into your tapestry a personal coevolutionary destiny? What do you feel about your potential to multi-perceptually select a more inclusionary and a love-guided world from the garden of your own sacred pure state?

---

55 Laszlo, *Science and the Akashic Field,* 140.

Chapter XIII
Conscious Evolutionary Weaving: Mystical Thought-Strands

Mystical apprehension of basic and limbic brain energetic feedback expresses a spiritual universal self-awareness. Our mystical thought-strands give examples of how non-local phenomena relate to us personally. The quotes provide answers to the question: what if we become weavers of the inner loom of multi-perceptual awareness? For example, how might one describe the experience of the impact of deciding to follow a golden thread calling? Our mystical thought-strands express in real terms the non-local coherent effect of a choice to respond when it could propagate in all directions at the same time. In addition to discovering the rest of your life could (non-locally) take care of itself, there are numerous transformational potentials for embodied universal self-awareness. The mystics illuminate what could collapse out of a virtual state. The inner garden of the subconscious is seeded with all possibilities that can be passionately apprehended—multi-perceptually.

Mystical Thought-Strand
Coevolutionary Perspective: We will begin weaving with Meister Eckhart whose understanding of the universal self is the *I AM, for all eternity*. Blessed are those who become fully aware. Jean-Yves Leloup describes the "blessing" when you receive *real support from*

the elements of nature. When the garden of the subconscious goes everywhere we do, it is possible to get into the dirt and touch the *non*-subjective root of a *subjective* passionate apprehension. At the foundation we can caress its potato-like nubs of the virtual states. A choice to tend one of the little nubs or seeds with the inner gardening or weaving process—could non-locally collapse, with help from *all elements of nature,* a world that a gnostic considers to be Paradise. It is the fruit and fabric of an integrated mind-body-heart complex.

Meister Eckhart:

> "Before I was born, I Am, for all eternity." Blessed are those who, while still in space-time, become conscious of their Being in eternity, for they are in this world but not of it, and even stones will serve them...When you are in harmony with the uncreated principle of all that is, then indeed all things seem to 'serve' you. There is a real support from all elements of nature. This is the gnostic view of Paradise.[56]

Mystical Thought-Strand

Coevolutionary Perspective: Gitta Mallasz and her friends lived in Hungary when the Nazi troops took control and occupied their country in October 1943. They experienced two transformational revelations that echo the inner loom's potential to select alternative physical realities to what they were facing—which reflects the lack of conscience in the separated mind. Mallasz saw the possibility of a *bridge* that could span the great abyss that divides the world created by Nazism and the creative world of virtual states. The bridge was given to us, she believed, and is

---

56 Leloup (Meister Eckhart paraphrases Yeshua's word 'Uncreated'), *The Gospel of Thomas: The Gnostic Wisdom of Jesus* (Rochester, VT: Inner Traditions, 2005), 94.

life-saving during times of extreme need. The bridge could symbolize a multi-perceptual awareness, when the same responsive way of relating also transforms us into embodied expressions of what is being related to, where unifying effects could proliferate in all directions at the same time. The second revelation, made multi-perceptually apparent, is the understanding that the radiance of creation lives in us. Gitta's mystical insights affirm we are never helpless.

Gitta Mallasz:

> The created world, and the creative world.
> Between the two: the Abyss.
> Be sure you understand this!
> You yourself are the bridge.
> It will not avail you to desire the radiance of creation,
> When you, within yourself, are the bridge.
> This has been given to you.[57]

Mystical Thought-Strand

Coevolutionary Perspective: Jean-Yves Leloup brings a clear understanding "what" constitutes the bridge, which has transformational potentials. It is when we become animated and coordinated expressions of a synthesis of personal and universal self-awareness. We metamorphize into an *archetype of synthesis*.

Jean-Yves Leloup:

> It is when we become bridges ourselves that we have the possibility to be both fully human and fully divine, in the

---

57 Gitta Mallasz, *Dialogue avec l'ange* (Aubier, 1996), cited by Jean-Yves Leloup, *The Gospel of Mary Magdalene* (Rochester, VT: Inner Traditions, 2002), 72.

image and the likeness of that which the ancients called the 'archetype of synthesis.'[58]

Conscious Evolutionary Gardening and Weaving—Indigenous to being Human:

The ancient Quiche Maya were aware of the agency that the processes of gardening and weaving have to manifest a new earth. They could have "offered up" their need for a homeland to the cyclic rhythm and patterns of gardening and weaving. The sensual and multi-perceptual processes could have drawn out the whole message described in the Ancient Word. In the same way that inner gardening and weaving could *select* a new earth, the ancient Quiche Maya could have experienced the same potential for their labors of love. The integrated lifestyle of the culture was a fractal of Nature's energetic and quantum coherent patterns. Barbara and Denis Tedlock give two interpretations of the opening lines of the sacred text, the Popol Vuh.[59]

First translation:

This is the beginning of the Ancient Word, here in this place called Quiche. Here we shall inscribe, we shall implant the Ancient Word.

Second interpretation:

Here we shall design, we shall brocade the Ancient Word.

---

58 Leloup, *The Gospel of Mary Magdalene*, 75.
59 Janet C. Berlo, *Beyond Bricolage: Women and Aesthetic Strategies in Latin American Textiles*, cites translations of first lines in Popol Vuh by Barbara and Denis Tedlock in an essay from anthology *The Textile Traditions of Mesoamerica and the Andes* (Austin, TX: University of Texas Press, 1996), 445.

~ Your LifeBook Journal

Conscious evolutionary gardening and weaving are two ways we could become a consequence of the transcendent and desire-prompted universal self-experiences. The mystics interpret the quantum aspect of our being as divine, and individuals such as Mallasz affirm there is a human link to a vast untapped reservoir of *virtually* everything separated thinking has been unable to imagine. A coevolutionary perspective is critical when it acknowledges the fact it is necessary to choose to respond to the instinctual and emotional cues. The great poet W. H. Auden expressed frustration when he said, "Poetry makes nothing happen,"[60] which affirms the typically inconsequential influence of a revelatory synthesis of multi-perceptual awareness. The garden of the subconscious and inner loom of multi-perceptual awareness may indeed have been given to us for implanting seeds of universal self-awareness or brocading its new earth fabric. A recurring theme of the book is "crossing the line." The threads of the evolutionary, conscious evolutionary, and coevolutionary perspectives are knotted with the fibers of personal experiences, now synthesized in the sacred space of Your LifeBook Journal. Let's pause and take stock of what has been revealed in the very big tapestry of thought for conscious evolutionary weaving. We wish to see the totality of information in order to determine what the sum of the different types of thought-strands can show us. The judge of this, however, is based on what is personally relevant, when everything the science strands describe is a part of who we are and a human potential to experience, reflect on, and possibly have an influence on or with its phenomena. Our tapestry has revealed a diamond in the rough, and it could be reclaimed as a rare jewel of being human and alive. First, make a list to identify what is stopping you from crossing the line. Place next to this, notes on the science-strands

---

[60] W. H. Auden, in *Remembering W.H. Auden*, Hannah Arendt ("A Critic at Large," January 20, 1975, republished in *The New Yorker Magazine*), Dec 3, 2018, 70.

you feel most support your multi-perceptual intuition; you have a role in the selecting of a future, which compares with the unitive perspective. Make another short list of which mystical revelations affirm this potential. Piece the lists together in any configuration or shape. Describe what you feel, think, and realize is true as they merge into a soft tissue of personal understanding. Has the texture of the collage moved you any closer, or even over the invisible line—which most balk at the point of asking, what if?

Chapter XIV
Unifying Our Universal Masculine and Feminine Principles

Have you ever noticed there is no such thing as a bored toddler? They know exactly what they want. If you watch them closely, it becomes apparent they are attracted to something definite but unseen like the children's birthday party game, "pinning the tail on the donkey." With an outstretched arm, paper tail and pin in hand, the child is blindfolded and then he or she is turned around three times before being set free. Completely disoriented, they strike out confidently with the full intention of pinning the tail on the picture of the donkey. This is a good analogy of what happens to most of us. We enter the world blindfolded with a great life-attraction, then get turned around by educations preparing us for less than what it means to be human and alive. Thus, a part of us remains a mystery as well as something goes unnoticed and its potential is a missing force in the world.

Marie Montessori would only follow a child up to a point. We have arrived at a human decision window beyond which the future is unknown. In the midst of everyday life activities, we are aware we have a relationship with the universe, but what it is has remained a mystery. We have been given warnings to change our way of life, but how or what must be done is unclear.

These gaps in the human experience reveal there is a big hole or sharp cliff, then a deep void drops without end. They all have something to do with universal self-experiences, which are considered out-of-the-ordinary. Over the course of the book, the fabrics of evolutionary, conscious evolutionary, and coevolutionary perspectives have materialized understanding of a latent coevolutionary purpose, but still a significant piece remains unaccounted for.

The Unwritten Book has been written in the spirit of "If you see something, say something." In the chapters for the third organic personal conscious evolution, *Unifying Our Universal Masculine and Feminine Principles,* I unveil the missing face of the feminine desire-prompted / process-based universal self-impulse and attraction. Nature, with whom she is related, is also feminine. The vibrations of the feminine voice reverberate with the transcendent *masculine* whole message through the multi-perceptual mind-body-heart complex. She is the feminine figure behind the primacy of the in-between—the middle earth, the middle ground, between waking consciousness and the transcendent self-awareness with a deep seated coevolutionary conscience. When we surrender to her call, whatever and however we respond will serve a greater good when it is how she can live us—being her.

Something more needs to be said about getting safely across the evolutionary crossroads, which depends on two reactions to her experience. They both have to do with her emotional attractive force. Her passionate apprehension or immaculate universal self-conception fuels the courage to take a leap of faith across the divide. The flight-pattern for leaping or migrating safely, as was illustrated with the story-mirror *The Snowstorm,* is a shift from a separated to a universal self-identity. Navigating the shift is a question of healing the trauma that separated thinking has inflicted on us personally with her love of intimacy, compassion, and humility. The feminine principle is at the helm with an expansive passionate apprehension and healing compassionate approach. These are both transportive qualities of love when the destinations are their transformational effects.

The masculine principle is associated with the transcendent; the wave-face; the undifferentiated whole; the whole message; the electromagnetic and thermodynamic patterns, the pure state; the domain of coherence—a superposition of all possibilities, he is one of the organizers in a coevolutionary partnership, and the Great What Is.

The feminine principle, however, also embraces the masculine, when his symbol is part of Nature. They form a dyad expressing the whole universal self-identity. Our true self reflects the twain. Animals in the wild instinctively become animated and coordinated holograms while the desire-prompted / process-based feminine impulse and attraction serves as the human guide. Therefore, her symbol includes relating multi-perceptually, also reacting to the presence of the transcendent masculine patterns that underlie our biology. She inspires taking a stand for our non-local wholeness by relating multi-perceptually. The responses organically guide a personal conscious evolution. The experience and influence of the feminine principle, therefore, forms the basis of the evolutionary, conscious evolutionary, and coevolutionary perspectives. These recognize there is something more to us than is being seen rationally, and it has a feminine face.

She gives us the potential to become universal self-conscious and guided. The reason why these are out-of-the-ordinary is because – like Nature who she represents – the feminine principle has not played a prominent role in human evolution. She is the I AM that calls us to become one unified masculine and feminine whole. This is who we truly are, but her half has rarely been acknowledged.

Jean-Yves Leloup expresses philosopher Karl Graf von Dürkheim's conscious evolutionary perspective, considering that the two principles need to be internalized for the sake of future well-being. Understanding multi-perceptually engages the whole brain by fully responding to feminine awareness of the transcendent, which influences transformations as part of its process of relating.

> In our age the recovery (or discovery) of the spiritual must occur through the reconciliation with the feminine. The

goal is the wedding of the masculine and the feminine: the Anthropos. This wedding must be initiated within us on a social level; on a neurophysiological level (the harmonization of the brain hemispheres); and on a more universal and planetary level.[61]

The third organic personal conscious evolution uses the analogy of a biological pregnancy as the experience of internalizing both. It is the feminine principle, however, who conceives, gestates, and births—not only Anthropos. Like the other two approaches, personally transformative, this one is also coevolutionary when the process allows Nature to evolve through us.

We will look at the potential to imagine multi-perceptually from two different positions. The first is in recognition that the morphology of our three brain systems, and the possibilities it represents, belongs to Nature. It is the wild that lives in us and she uses our imagination to transform with an integrated masculine and feminine consciousness. When Nature's creative force evolves with multi-perceptual awareness, she becomes the muse. This is also an example of her tendency to be opportunistic with our power to imagine. Gestating what she wants to express has its own unique existential crisis. The imagining is never subjective and always is creational or physically transformational. We do not have a choice in what she desires to express, and its *seed* belongs to the masculine organizer. When we respond to her call, it is how we follow through with symmetrical coupling with the masculine principle. This is another way to describe an integrated multi-perceptual response, which includes the conscious evolutionary interface, or *gestating personal alignment,* with his ecological patterns. The marriage between the universal feminine and masculine principles ensures what comes into form, or the baby, is *theirs,* and not the offspring of the separated mind, who conceptualizes without the

---

[61] Leloup, *The Gospel of Mary Magdalene,* 164-165.

feminine embodying or gestating process so critical to ecological compatibility.

Nature may borrow a human multi-perceptual awareness for her coevolutionary purpose. Or, we could fulfill the uniquely human potential to become universal self-conscious, which serves the same impersonal function and is also personally transformative. In this case, a response to an out-of-the-ordinary universal self-experience becomes a coevolutionary contribution, when multi-perceptually conceived, gestated, and birthed.

Meister Eckhart reveals the potency of the multi-perceptual feminine *one-eye*. It is also her womb—and the garden of the subconscious, as well as the inner loom, which becomes activated by her passionate apprehension. Her integrated *organ of insight* is therefore highly "versatile." It is both / and, our eye and Nature's. When we respond it is *both* the whole message *and* the medium of expression. *The eye with which I see God is the eye with which God sees me: one vision, one knowledge, one love.*[62]

The trimesters of a conscious evolutionary pregnancy, from both perspectives, include pre-conception / conception, gestation, and birth. I will weave a tapestry of thought, beginning with showing when Nature is the muse and she is looking through the one-eye of multi-perceptual awareness. It will be referred to as the *upper fabric*. It includes yarns from a coevolutionary perspective and philosophical thought-strands. The tapestry will also integrate Sophia thought-strands. They draw from a patchwork of myths that reveal the divine feminine as Sophia. She captures the transformational or coevolutionary focus of the desire-prompted / process-based feminine universal self-impulse and attraction. Interestingly, the word *philosophy* means love of Sophia—philo-Sophia. It is noteworthy when the highly rationally-minded philosophers would never imagine "abandoning" their imaginations or one-eye to Nature

---

62 Eckhart (cited by Leloup), *The Gospel of Thomas* (Rochester, VT: Inner Traditions, 2005), 73.

who has languished behind the mask of an inconsequential myth. Nevertheless... *she not only forms the earth and heaven of the retort that we call life, and is not only the whirling wheel revolving within it, but is also the supreme essence and distillation to which life in this world can be transformed.*[63]

The lower fabric will use the ancient Greek compound revelation *Apokalupsis, Parousia, Gnosis* to describe a personal universal self-conception. I will exchange the philosophical thought-strands for Jean-Yves Leloup's interpretations for the three Greek revelations. I will continue with the coevolutionary perspective and the Sophia fibers. These twist together to form the through-line thread between the upper and lower fabrics. They unify our universal masculine and feminine principles on both sides of the one-eye.

The theme of unifying male and female in a conscious evolutionary pregnancy offers the first *immaculate universal self-conception sex-ed primer.* It is a coevolutionary, non-physical, non-gender-specific, but feminine-guided embodying of the transcendent masculine whole message. The upper fabric describes the symptoms of the trimesters when we are conceiving, gestating, and birthing Nature's wild imagination. The second portion of the tapestry describes the signs of each trimester when we have become pregnant with a personal universal self-conception. The purpose of the primer is to support choosing to enter each new phase of conception, gestation, and birth. This becomes more likely if you can identify the signs of each trimester, and fully appreciate the transformational potentials as well as their existential challenges. Identifying these and placing them in the joyful context of a pregnancy, simultaneously creates transparency with the steep coevolutionary learning curve of a conscious evolutionary pregnancy, while at the same time, there is a hopeful sense of expectancy.

Existential discomfort is also felt with inner gardening and weaving. The severity of the *contractions* is why the question *What if?*

---

[63] Erich Neumann, *The Great Mother* (Princeton, NJ: Princeton University Press, 1955), 325.

persists and has yet to be answered. Its invisible line has rarely been crossed; therefore the history of what could happen has remained unknown, unlived, and unwritten. If the difficulties could become *a sign*, when a future that truly feels like a fit is as close as an embodied, pregnant understanding, maybe the discomforts could almost be an opportunity to influence a transformational impact—in all directions at the same time.

~ Your LifeBook Journal

The whiff of silence from the garden of the subconscious is the imperceptible but palpable feminine principle. She has lived under the radar, when her multi-perceptual imagination can be adapted to serving the purposes of the separated mind. She is the wild world inside of us and our multi-perceptual imagination belongs to Nature. It is *both* the eye with which we see the universal self, *and* the eye through which Nature sees us acting on her evolutionary behalf. How liberated is your wild imagination? Would you consider sharing it with her?

Chapter XV
Upper Fabric: Immaculate Universal Self-Conception Sex-Ed Primer: Imagining with Nature

Imagine you had no idea you were pregnant and were completely unaware of the symptoms. Just think of how you might feel as your belly begins to expand and suddenly you are in labor! Fortunately, the trimesters of a physical pregnancy are clearly presented with many sex educations. There are no equivalents, however, for when you become pregnant with a transformational multi-perceptual synthesis. The immaculate universal self sex-ed primer identifies the coevolutionary trimesters, whether you are experiencing Nature imagining *with you* or you undergo a personal universal self-conception. In either case, feminine love guides, embodying the whole message of our masculine and feminine universal self. Let us begin making connections with the symptoms when Nature wishes to imagine with us. We will try to conceive, gestate, and birth likenesses to the imagination of a synthesis of masculine and feminine multi-perceptual awareness.

First Trimester: Pre-Conception
Coevolutionary Perspective: Something takes over our senses. Whatever it is feels like a huge potential. It produces anxiety when its promise of becoming fulfilled seems way out of our

league. Yet, accompanying the overwhelming sensation is experiencing one's great mystery. It seems as if the potential has chosen us, who will conceive, gestate, and birth its expression into the world. Pre-conception is a dynamic feeling of the primacy of the in-between. It is where the life force in our cells is stirring. Pre-conception is an intense unitive experience with the force of creation. You feel the whirling wheel of Nature's muse beginning to animate your imagination. Awareness grows about the potential that knowing and living the meaning of the experience is also excruciating when it escapes comprehension. Our philosopher thought-strand affirms the comprehensiveness or all-ness of a synthesis of pre-conceptualized multi-perceptual awareness. Its raw imagination is transcendent but valued as a human faculty, blind but indispensable. Even the pragmatist Emmanuel Kant, in his Critique of Pure Reason, was aware of its potency to generate new understandings.

Philosophical Thought-Strand

> Synthesis in general is [...] the simple effect of the imagination, that is to say, of a human faculty that is blind but indispensable, and without which we could never have any sort of knowledge, though we are only very rarely aware of this.[64]

Pre-Conception

Sophia Thought-Strand: The Sophia strand expresses the creational, transformational, and whole-oriented purpose of our inner feminine. Pre-conception includes the experience of her life-affirming and coevolutionary principle as our own life force. A sign that Nature is guiding the pregnancy is when a multi-perceptual synthesis evokes a haunting experience of your eternal unity in the totality of Nature's universe. Its meaning is beyond comprehension

---

64 Emmanuel Kant, cited in *The Gospel of Mary Magdalene,* Jean-Yves Leloup (Rochester, VT: Inner Traditions International, 2002), 126.

because you are in a phase of pre-conception. Something will speak to you at conception, which then can be gestated. It is critical at this early stage of a conscious evolutionary pregnancy to respond by choosing to wait for a passionate apprehension.

Sophia Thought-Strand

> We find that in its elementary and transformative character, the Feminine as "creative principle" encompasses the whole world. This is the totality of nature in its original unity, from which all life arises and unfolds, assuming, in its highest transformation, the form of the spirit.[65]

Conception: Philosophical Thought-Strand

Coevolutionary Perspective: When Nature seeks to imagine with us, the symptom is a passionate desire to apprehend meaning in the blind imagination of a synthesis. The sign you are experiencing an immaculate conception is an intense body-awareness of the masculine whole message regarding his pattern interdependence. It is a transcendent apperception of the truth—we are mutually related and mutually defining. You know you are experiencing conception when, as Hellenistic philosopher Plotinus (c. 204-270) phrases it, you

> …see all things, not in process of becoming, but in Being, and see [yourself] in the other. Each being contains in itself the whole intelligible world. Therefore, All is everywhere. Each are All, and All is each. Man as he now is has ceased to be the All. But when he ceases to be an individual, he raises himself again and penetrates the whole world.[66]

---

65 Neumann, 62.
66 Aldous Huxley, *The Perennial Philosophy*, cites Plotinus, 5.

Conception

Sophia Thought-Strand: Sophia expresses the impersonal aspect of Nature. She is not really interested in "mothering." Her compassionate impulse is not to coddle, but rather to support a metamorphosis, as we conceive and incarnate our masculine principle's whole message. A symptom of conception is awareness that your life is not really your own when it is her transformational or evolutionary pathway. Her unifying purpose is uncompromising. She is less concerned for the immense personal conscious evolution that we must undertake in order to fully respond. This expresses our feminine principle's *tough love*. There are no guarantees when we come under her influence, but then again ... *her overflowing heart is wisdom and food at once.*

Sophia Thought-Strand

> Thus, the spiritual power of Sophia is living and saving; her overflowing heart is wisdom and food at once. The nourishing life that she communicates is a life of the spirit and of transformation, not one of earthbound materiality. As spirit mother, she is not, like the Great Mother of the lower phase, interested primarily in the infant, the child, and the immature man, who cling to her in these stages. She is rather a goddess of the Whole, who governs the transformation from the elementary to the spiritual level; who desires whole men knowing life in all its breadth, from the elementary phase to the phase of spiritual transformation.[67]

Second Trimester

Gestation: Philosopher Thought-Strand

Philosophers Christian Jambet and Martin Heidegger describe the experience of the subtle but nonetheless earthshattering

---

[67] Neumann, 331.

realization of what Nature has in mind—for us. We have never experienced the world like a salamander, turtle, or chipmunk where *all parts respond to the rest of the world as a whole, maintain themselves as a whole, and change and evolve as a whole*. A symptom of the second trimester is "morning sickness" as we enter the womb in between the created reality and the creative realm of gestation. The philosophers acknowledge the environment of the womb is beyond comprehension. Its *place is close to the ultimate root of subjectivity: transcendental apperception, which unifies the totality of the given and the edifice of judgments*. The trimester gestation is symbolic of transitioning to a new multi-perceptually responsive life. We also become aware we are gestating our butterfly. The metamorphosis, however, looks more like a new place of human interdependence—a new earth, which becomes gestated by symmetrical coupling between our masculine and feminine principles of Nature. She is imagining with us, and this is making us pregnant, where the symptom of morning sickness is brought on by a highly disturbing intuition that a *transcendental imagination is without a homeland*. We are gestating a coevolutionary unknown. Nature has faith in our ability to collapse or birth a physical likeness to what she is imagining, but it will express a unique embodied response. As foreign as this potential is in a world that does not unify masculine and feminine principles, it is the coevolutionary purpose with which we came into the world—ready to pin the tail on its donkey.

> It is clear that the 'blind' imagination is for us dark, hidden, and mute, for it does not reveal anything in particular to us, and especially nothing imaginary. It gives nothing more than the world, and just the world. Its place is close to the ultimate root of subjectivity: transcendental apperception, which unifies the totality of the given and the edifice of judgments. This place is so enigmatic that Heidegger, meditating upon the most famous passages of the *Critique*,

coined this most striking résumé: "The transcendental imagination is without a homeland."[68]

Gestation

Sophia Thought-Strand: The gnostic Sophia Thought-Strand presents three images of our feminine principle's *gestating womb*—wherein a transcendental apperception becomes embodied. She is the highest Godhead—a dyad of masculine and feminine principles. In this marriage she is viewed as an eternal Mystic Silence—whose fertile essence of a new earth seed was intimately experienced with inner gardening. The divine feminine is also associated with the Holy Spirit in the Holy Trinity. She governs the gestating or incarnating of the Godhead—a response to the sense and texture of the *totality of the given*, the masculine and feminine larger whole. A multi-perceptual apperception entrains its feminine focus at the bare-root level of human subjectivity. It is the womb of the primacy of the in-between, where the non-living and impersonal masculine ecological patterns, such as interdependence, resonate with the feminine energetically. Our non-verbal emotional response intimately animates Holy Sophia. She is the attractive coevolutionary force and stabilizing conscience of a mind-body-heart integration during gestation and birth.

> There are three principal characterizations of the divine feminine in early Gnostic writings. The first of these perceives the highest Godhead as a dyad of masculine and feminine elements, wherein the feminine component is represented as an eternal, mystic Silence. The second sees the Holy Spirit as feminine, thus including the female element in the Holy Trinity, which in most Gnostic myths represents

---

68 Christian Jambet, *La Logique des Orientaux,* 60, cited by Leloup in *The Gospel of Mary Magdalene,* 126.

the Godhead in manifestation. The third is the characterization of the Holy Sophia...[69]

Third Trimester

Birth: Philosophical Thought-Strand

Coevolutionary Perspective: The butterfly emerging from the womb of gestation may be identified as the human Anthropos. However, our true self mirrors the world that an integrated mind-body-heart synthesis coevolves, manifests, collapses, or births. The embodied awareness is the pure energy of goodness, truth, and beauty, maintaining the non-subjective quality of wholeness of a multi-perceptual synthesis. What becomes born is the possible *destination* of what has persisted as *a homeless imagination*. The symptom of birth is an impulse to completely surrender to *delivering* the unknown child or homeland, which is free of hypocrisy, extremism, and meaninglessness.

Philosophical Thought-Strand:

> Gnosis is a force, not just a set of ideas, symbols, or concepts... This deeper knowing may properly be called pure consciousness—or perhaps more precisely, the pure energy of consciousness. It is an energy, no doubt itself existing at many levels, that can be allowed to descend into the body, heart, and mind and, through its own active force, make of us the being called *anthropos*, the awakened, fully human being.[70]

---

69 Violet MacDermot, *The Fall of Sophia: A Gnostic Text on the Redemption of Universal Consciousness* (Great Barrington, MA: Lindisfarne Books, 2001), 10.
70 Jacob Needleman, foreword to *The Gospel of Thomas* by Jean-Yves Leloup (Rochester, VT: Inner Traditions, 1986), ix-x.

Sophia Thought-Strand: As challenging as gestation is, the conscious evolutionary healing process cleanses, clears, and reclaims a sustainable future. From the sacred space of the in-between – or womb, vessel, cocoon – we re-emerge free of the materialistic caterpillar self along with a new homeland that is tucked under its wing. The butterfly and its world are "re-enchantments" with infusions of love, the possibilities of which are uncorrupted by separated thinking.

Sophia Thought-Strand

> The feminine vessel as vessel of rebirth and higher transformation becomes Sophia and the Holy Ghost. It not only... receives that which is to be transformed, in order to spiritualize and deify it, but is also the power that nourishes what has been transformed and reborn.[71]

~ Your LifeBook Journal

Choosing to imagine as Nature, who is thinking with us, makes us pregnant with an inclusionary rather than exclusionary world. The immaculate universal self-conception sex-ed primer, for when Nature is seeing as us, is an essential guide. That which can be responded to multi-perceptually is allowed to gestate and become born. Rarely do we see ourselves as evolutionary pathways, perhaps because the experience of the universal masculine and feminine goes undetected, neither recognized nor identified with. When they are sensed and felt as an inner unity, it is impossible to not know the truth. We are part of life and have the purpose, as is true of all species, to support its continuance as a labor of love. Becoming pregnant with the immaculate conception of interdependence, *which unifies the totality of the given and the edifice of judgments,* is a gift to the world and to ourselves. The homelessness that we see

---

71 Neumann, 329.

in the world is a painful mirroring of the alienation from our true being, our separation from the rest of the world, and the way we think—blocking a purpose that we were born ready to serve. Can you imagine choosing to relate multi-perceptually through all of its trimesters? Can you see how in one fell swoop it could—you could: end homelessness, prevent habitat loss for all human and creature life dancers, and possibly destroy (turn over) everything that is exclusionary—not violently, but simply as James Baldwin astutely understood, the crises would no longer be needed if you choose to think with the heart? How near or far away do you think *we are*, from the homeland of your transcendental imagination, based on how ready *you are* to embrace your masculine and feminine principles?

Chapter XVI
Lower Fabric: A Universal Self-Conception

A conscious evolutionary pregnancy, which gestates a blind imagination with Nature, or when we assimilate a universal self-conception, both pregnancies serve the impersonal, non-human coevolutionary purpose. However, its impulse and attraction are supremely meaningful, as evidenced by descriptions of its pursuit, to be the Pearl Beyond Price. The two types of conscious evolutionary pregnancies are guided by our feminine principle's passionate and compassionate, tough-love responses to Nature's coevolutionary purpose. Therefore, the existentially apocalyptic aspect of all organic personal conscious evolutions, relates to the psychological impacts of a multi-perceptual synthesis of a non-subjective whole message and coevolutionary human purpose. However, while inner chaos is being felt, a unified feminine experience simultaneously renews and re-enchants with experiences of waves of love. Of the two polar opposite experiences, the primer supports responding to the ones that evoke tsunamis of empathy—even though a multi-perceptual imagination feels homeless and hopeless from common separated perspectives. The apocalyptic coronavirus has liberated the universal feminine principle from the cracks of a shattered world. A universal self-conception is a highly potent embodied observation; it could virtually transform everything as our feminine principle gets involved.

Let us continue weaving the lower fabric of the immaculate universal self sex-ed primer, using the compound ancient Greek revelation—Apokalupsis, Parousia, Gnosis. Each of the three epiphanies corresponds with pre-conception / conception, gestation, and birth. The tapestry continues with the coevolutionary perspective and Sophia thought-strands. We will exchange the philosophical thought-strands of the upper fabric for Jean-Yves Leloup's explanations of the Apokalupsis, Parousia, Gnosis illuminations and continue to weave in the coevolutionary perspective and Sophia thought-strands. These maintain a connection with the evolutionary role our feminine principle could play with birthing an ecologically-based civilization from the womb of an integrated mind—and body and heart.

Making eye contact with Nature, with whom we share the one-eye, could trigger a double universal self-conception. This would take place when we are both looking through the one-eye of multi-perceptual awareness at each other, at the same time. Were a process of relating, which includes becoming an integrated archetype of synthesis, to become normalized, another great mystery would be: the potential of a double universal self-conception. Could it morph into a super-womb or coevolutionary Godhead? Our Sophia thought-strand, symbolizing the wild in us, will reveal this extraordinary possibility in the conscious evolutionary trimester at birth.

Apokalupsis

Coevolutionary Perspective: The point at which a golden thread calling – or any emotional out-of-the-ordinary universal self-awareness – becomes apprehended, it is a sign for pre-conception / conception or the Apokalupsis. It is a light-filled spontaneous receiving of the whole message. It is joyful and hopeful, because it is eternal. However, the word Apokalupsis underscores the psychological impacts of two prominent features of the masculine / feminine dyad expressing our total universal self-identity. A sensuous and tactile unified male and female experience is pre-conception and conception taking place simultaneously. Apokalupsis is the realization of a transcendental apperception—*both* the experience of a synthesis *and* its epiphany—there is no separation between masculine and feminine principles and the living world, which reflects their union. Thus, this trimester includes the existentially challenging revelation of the impersonal, non-subjective, and transcendent masculine wave-face and our feminine principle, known by her overflowing experience of Love. The whole message of pre-conception / conception is a shocker when it is realized *how much time we have wasted playing in the shadows*—instead of choosing to act from our hearts; this realization moment organically mirrors the transcendent pure state. The two experiences – an immaculate conception of the fullness of our true being *and* an impoverished physical identity, a life where our feminine face of love has been overshadowed by business-as-usual concerns – are positive symptoms—a sign the trimester pre-conception / conception is taking place. The juxtaposition between the two awakenings also captures the uphill / downhill thermodynamics of a desire-prompted personal conscious evolution. If you did not know these were normal experiences for a species, whose gift to the world is embodied universal self-awareness, its potential would most likely miscarry.

Apokalupsis

> The day of the Apocalypse is the day of the Unveiling of What Is[72]... The day of the Apocalypse is also the day when the reality of God is revealed to us. The First Letter of John says: "Then we will be like him, for we will see him as he is." Is it a joyful day, or a terrible one? We will see Love and we will also see how little we have loved. We will see that we are living beings who come from the Living One and see also how little we have rejoiced in this. We will see that we are

---

72 Leloup, *The Gospel of Thomas*, 216.

light born of the Light and we will see how much time we have wasted playing in the shadows.[73]

Sophia Thought-Strand: Our feminine principle is the bridge (we have been given) between the stark and cold non-local realm of the masculine principle and us, who live in space-time. When the coevolutionary feminine is responded to, the masculine principle in us also becomes apparent. The combined self-experiences automatically inspire the apocalyptic realization: we are not who we thought we were. Our multi-perceptual feminine not only shows tough love by not sparing us the truth. She also guides the reconciling process with intimacy, compassion, and humility. Our feminine principle, therefore, is the wild, pure expression of love, and she is also the uncompromising *bride of the Apocalypse.*

Sophia Thought-Strand:

> Sophia is also the 'spirit and the bride' of the Apocalypse, of whom it is written: "And let him that is athirst come. And whosoever will, let him take the water of life freely."[74]

Second Revelation

Parousia

Coevolutionary Perspective: Parousia is a daring choice to gestate the information received at conception. It is risky because we cross the line that is rarely traversed by giving ourselves permission to respond to the Apokalupsis. The evolutionary significance, however, is: we end the world that mirrors a lack of response to the sensation of the presence of the whole self. The corona crisis may have already accomplished its demise. However, we have to decide whether to rebuild with separated thinking or lay claim to the lost feminine

---

73 Ibid.
74 Neumann, 329.

principle of coevolution. A decision to gestate the experience – all lives matter, for example – is how we become evolutionary pathways to virtually everything that is multi-perceptually possible, to collapse, manifest, or birth into form. Therefore, the day we see the whole masculine and feminine universal self-identity is also the day its presence and coevolutionary *final cause – the Plenitude and Presence that are always calling us* – is intimately felt and taken up as a golden thread purpose. Parousia is a sign that you are choosing a non-linear, non-subjective, and dual masculine and feminine coevolutionary cause. Our feminine principle, who is the face of love and Nature, is the *causal force* of human coevolution. A conscious evolutionary pregnancy relies on the feminine art of flowing from a passionate apprehending into the womb of an intimate, compassionate, and humble embodiment of our whole masculine and feminine being. Gestation, therefore, is when we become bridges—archetypes of synthesis (our transparent butterfly version) who mirror what Jean-Yves Leloup previously described as both human and divine aspects of humanity.

Parousia:

> The day of the Apocalypse is also the day of Parousia. The Greek word *parousia* means 'presence.' Neither of these terms is reserved to refer to some future return of Christ—that is, the Second Coming at the end of time. We can already experience moments of parousia when the Presence makes itself totally felt in us. "It fills all; it is not I who live, but Christ in me," as Paul said…A holy being is someone filled with the Spirit, completely inhabited by the Presence of Love. Such a being is already the incarnation of the end of the world and the end of humanity—that is to say, the goal and final cause, the Plenitude and Presence that are always calling us.[75]

---

75 Leloup, *The Gospel of Thomas*, 217.

Sophia Thought-Strand: The cataclysmic aspect – both / and, the Apokalupsis-Parousia revelations – is the effect of the multi-perceptual feminine principle getting involved—even if her intervention goes unmentioned by Leloup. The world we live in has a masculine face, which is associated with rational thinking. The prevailing misconception, and the world that it has produced, views the masculine principle as dominant. Exposed is a big hole in a rational understanding, which leads to schisms in all areas of human existence. A choice to surrender to our gestating feminine could heal the misconception, at the same time that unifying both principles could gestate the transformation of an unbalanced world into one that is whole and healthy.

Sophia Thought-Strand

> The matriarchal world is geocentric in the comprehensive sense that tangible, visible reality is the source even of its highest manifestations, namely, the spiritual phenomena that arise in it. In the matriarchal world the woman as vessel is not made by man or out of man or used for his procreative purposes; rather, the reverse is true: it is this vessel with its mysterious creative character that brings forth the male in itself and from out of itself... in the matriarchate man is looked upon as a sower, but he did not perceive the radical meaning of this image, in which the man is only an instrument of the earth and the seed he sows is not "his" seed but earth seed.[76]

Gnosis

Coevolutionary Perspective: At the same time a universal self-witnessing takes place, we also sense the presence of its wave-face, and at this very moment, also know it is our truth. Gnosis is the

---

76 Neumann, 62.

fulfillment of a coevolutionary, conscious evolutionary pregnancy. A choice to take a leap of faith – trusting in embodied transcendent and universal feminine awareness – has a hormonal effect that starts labor. The contracting and expanding labor pains are felt as they begin to bear down. The symptoms are manifold. We are letting go of what was familiar, but the future is unclear. This is an apocalyptic labor pain. Its trauma is compounded by the realization: the entire pregnancy has been in service to an impersonal coevolutionary purpose. The baby that we have been gestating is not ours, and this is a painful empty nest experience before the child has even arrived. The form the baby will take is unknown. It could be the ephemeral coevolutionary butterfly—the archetype of synthesis, who multi-tasks as the bridge to an alternative destination to a planetary Armageddon. There are no more masks of separation to obstruct the birth canal of our love-guided feminine. Gnosis is the fulfillment of the first two revelations, which is also the acquiring of a human potential to become universal self-conscious and guided.

Gnosis:

> *Gnosis* is the recognition of the Self. It alone makes possible the realization of the Apocalypse and Parousia in the true sense of these words. Self-knowledge is indeed a process of apokalupsis, of progressive unveiling, one mask dropping after another, from apocalypse to apocalypse. This is how we discover ourselves as we truly are.[77]

Sophia Thought-Strand: Double universal self-conception is possible when a personally animated expression of the larger whole becomes the one-eye that Sophia sees as her dyad of coevolutionary / transformational principles. We reflect the *new bi-identity* (masculine and

---

77 Leloup, *The Gospel of Thomas*, 217.

feminine, organizer and organized)—*one invisible agent* or coevolutionary Godhead.

Sophia Thought-Strand:

> The new message is the gospel of identity. It is not an effort to unite lives in a common interest, but rather a recognition of the fact that all forms are manifestations of one invisible agent.[78]

A biological flaw in modern humans:

The sixth mass extinction has been influenced by the effects of unintegrated thinking. This way of relating evolved with a choice to no longer identify with Nature, which gave rise to an exploitative purpose. Long before this, however, at the origin of our species, there was a marked tendency to cause extinctions.

According to the "Out of Africa"[79] theory, *modern* humans originated from a small group in Africa about 200,000 years ago. Approximately 50,000 years in the past, a subset moved into Eurasia and as they traveled north and east, modern humans came into contact with Neanderthals and other "archaic humans." These hominids – along with Australia's giant marsupials, and the mega fauna of North America as well as New Zealand's moas – went extinct in their wake. Fast forward to today. Most of the great apes, polar bears, and many other species, mainly due to habitat loss on account of human activities, are on the verge of extinction. The director of the Institute for Evolutionary Anthropology's studies of human evolution, Jean-Jacques Hublin, explains, *"We don't have much evidence that the Neanderthals or other archaic humans ever led to*

---

78 MacDermot, *The Fall of Sophia: A Gnostic Text on the Redemption of Universal Consciousness,* quotes Manly P. Hall (Great Barrington, MA: Lindisfarne Books, 2001), 98.
79 Elizabeth Kolbert, "Sleeping with the Enemy," *The New Yorker Magazine,* August 15 &22, 2011, 64.

an extinction of a species of mammal or anything else. For modern humans, there are hundreds of examples, and we do it very well."[80]

Implied clearly, the feminine love-guided principle has been a much weaker evolutionary force than the impulse to control and dominate. A choice to respond, therefore, is not only radical but revolutionary. My mother inspires with her conscious evolutionary perspective—we have the right and responsibility to choose a humanizing and life-affirming future. The most important choice to this end: become who we truly are. To conceptualize, gestate, and birth—we surrender to a love affair between our two universal principles. A coevolved sustainable future is the manifestation of one invisible agent: *both* masculine and feminine. The immaculate universal self-conception primer is a coevolutionary guide in the reconciling of the already developed masculine principle with the ignored transformational and love-guided feminine. She is the wild I AM within, calling us to be who we truly are—an expression of Nature's oneness.

~ Your LifeBook Journal

Why is it, or how is it—we come into the world ready to coevolve rather than cause extinctions? This can only be answered personally when there are no coevolutionary perspectives to explain why we *know this is our purpose.* Before it can be discovered, we are turned away from the golden thread of a coevolutionary lifestyle, by a world that supports individualistic pursuits. It is based on the long unknown, yet to be lived, and unwritten history of individuals, who like ourselves, wonder about the meaning of out-of-the-ordinary universal self-experiences. Over the course of the book we have developed perspectives, which together represent a new beginning or origin of multi-perceptual humans. An example of the tough love expressed by the universal feminine is: she leaves our survival completely up to us. She is not going to coddle humans

---

80 Ibid., 74-75.

into learning how to weave their inner loom of multi-perceptual awareness. Her experiment: will we choose to surrender to our love experience of her presence within us? We have a choice to perish by remaining a victim of a biological flaw or survive by cultivating a latent potential to think-with, become-with, and make-kin[81] with Nature—which in order to do, will require high doses of feminine passion, intimacy, compassion, and humility.

We may not be able to avoid an apocalypse, but what kind it will be could be a choice. To remain influenced by the way the separated mind thinks could result in a full-blown mass extinction. On the other hand, a choice to surrender to the love-guided feminine principle is to receive our wounded parts, and by extension of these, also take in the fragmented world, to become transformed in her oozy primordial coevolutionary womb. The final question in the Unwritten Book is the one that was asked at the beginning. A fuller understanding could make all the difference in the world when its gnosis supports a willing response. Who are we before we became the person we identify with? Can you give an answer based on what has come to light? Can you identify with the one invisible agent, that in the process of honoring it, you no longer reflect a human experiment of Nature? As you disappear into the Mystic Silence of her multi-perceptual womb, you may reemerge to a world that is animated and coordinated with a whole message of love—that got lost a long time ago.

---

81 Donna Haraway, *Staying with the Trouble: Making Kin in the Chthulucene* (Durham and London: Duke University Press, 2016), 12-13.

About Suzanne

The journey of becoming an artist, author, and teacher has revealed more about myself and the meaning of my life than any accomplishments along the way. One story begins with realizing, as a young child, that I was an artist. When my focus became weaving, I took the necessary steps to eventually be proficient at the craft. I was introduced to weaving in Nantucket, Massachusetts, by Swedish weaver Marguretta Grandin-Nettles. I decided to study weaving in Sweden at the renowned craft schools, Säterglantan in Injon and Capellagården in Öland. Three years later I returned to the U.S. where I began a career weaving tapestry commissions, rugs, and textiles for the home. I have exhibited in museums and galleries and taught workshops in Swedish weaving techniques. I moved from Nantucket to Sweden, then Washington, D.C., and Takoma Park, Maryland, and today I reside with my husband on Vashon Island in Washington state. The subtext to this first story: while pursuing a career in art, I discovered my golden thread calling – my true purpose – is creating wholeness. Everything I learned from my first story fueled my curiosity and decision to find out what was influencing me to pursue a focus that was more a labor of love than a wise business decision. A new chapter of my life began when I seriously reflected on my experiences of the craft.

The cyclic integrative patterns of weaving create whole fabrics, which is also true of Nature's process of weaving the web of life. I learned the wisdom of the unwritten book from an artform, where the main concern is every strand contributing to the whole fabric.

The more I wove, I saw how each fiber is *both* a single thread in a textile *and* the whole cloth that it weaves. This developed into a tactile or multi-perceptual, *evolutionary perspective*. Today I relate to people as having a similar story to mine—we find our way in the world with all of its challenges, and I also see the uncelebrated story or subtext to the main story. It is the tale of unexpectedly sensing and feeling the whole fabric that we are part of and eternally express as our true being. It has taken me twenty-four years and many seasons and cycles of weaving fabrics and weaving thought-strands together to integrate those strands into what has become *The Unwritten Book: An Organic Personal Conscious Evolution*.

www.ingramcontent.com/pod-product-compliance
Lightning Source LLC
LaVergne TN
LVHW011422080426
835512LV00005B/221